AI Self-Driving Cars Inventiveness

Practical Advances in
Artificial Intelligence and Machine Learning

Dr. Lance B. Eliot, MBA, PhD

ISBN: 1-7329760-3-1
ISBN-13: 978-1-7329760-3-0

DEDICATION

To my incredible daughter, Lauren, and my incredible son, Michael.

Forest fortuna adiuvat (from the Latin; good fortune favors the brave).

CONTENTS

Lance B. Eliot

ACKNOWLEDGMENTS

I have been the beneficiary of advice and counsel by many friends, colleagues, family, investors, and many others. I want to thank everyone that has aided me throughout my career. I write from the heart and the head, having experienced first-hand what it means to have others around you that support you during the good times and the tough times.

To Warren Bennis, one of my doctoral advisors and ultimately a colleague, I offer my deepest thanks and appreciation, especially for his calm and insightful wisdom and support.

To Mark Stevens and his generous efforts toward funding and supporting the USC Stevens Center for Innovation.

To Lloyd Greif and the USC Lloyd Greif Center for Entrepreneurial Studies for their ongoing encouragement of founders and entrepreneurs.

To Peter Drucker, William Wang, Aaron Levie, Peter Kim, Jon Kraft, Cindy Crawford, Jenny Ming, Steve Milligan, Chis Underwood, Frank Gehry, Buzz Aldrin, Steve Forbes, Bill Thompson, Dave Dillon, Alan Fuerstman, Larry Ellison, Jim Sinegal, John Sperling, Mark Stevenson, Anand Nallathambi, Thomas Barrack, Jr., and many other innovators and leaders that I have met and gained mightily from doing so.

Thanks to Ed Trainor, Kevin Anderson, James Hickey, Wendell Jones, Ken Harris, DuWayne Peterson, Mike Brown, Jim Thornton, Abhi Beniwal, Al Biland, John Nomura, Eliot Weinman, John Desmond, and many others for their unwavering support during my career.

And most of all thanks as always to Michael and Lauren, for their ongoing support and for having seen me writing and heard much of this material during the many months involved in writing it. To their patience and willingness to listen.

Lance B. Eliot

INTRODUCTION

This is a book that provides the newest innovations and the latest Artificial Intelligence (AI) advances about the emerging nature of AI-based autonomous self-driving driverless cars. Via recent advances in Artificial Intelligence (AI) and Machine Learning (ML), we are nearing the day when vehicles can control themselves and will not require and nor rely upon human intervention to perform their driving tasks (or, that allow for human intervention, but only *require* human intervention in very limited ways).

Similar to my other related books, which I describe in a moment and list the chapters in the Appendix A of this book, I am particularly focused on those advances that pertain to self-driving cars. The phrase "autonomous vehicles" is often used to refer to any kind of vehicle, whether it is ground-based or in the air or sea, and whether it is a cargo hauling trailer truck or a conventional passenger car. Though the aspects described in this book are certainly applicable to all kinds of autonomous vehicles, I am focused more so here on cars.

Indeed, I am especially known for my role in aiding the advancement of self-driving cars, serving currently as the Executive Director of the Cybernetic Self-Driving Cars Institute.. In addition to writing software, designing and developing systems and software for self-driving cars, I also speak and write quite a bit about the topic. This book is a collection of some of my more advanced essays. For those of you that might have seen my essays posted elsewhere, I have updated them and integrated them into this book as one handy cohesive package.

You might be interested in companion books that I have written that provide additional key innovations and fundamentals about self-driving cars. Those books are entitled **"Introduction to Driverless Self-Driving Cars,"** **"Advances in AI and Autonomous Vehicles: Cybernetic Self-Driving Cars,"** **"Self-Driving Cars: "The Mother of All AI Projects,"** **"Innovation and Thought Leadership on Self-Driving Driverless Cars,"** **"New Advances in AI Autonomous Driverless Self-Driving Cars,"** and **"Autonomous Vehicle Driverless Self-Driving Cars and**

Artificial Intelligence," "Transformative Artificial Intelligence Driverless Self-Driving Cars," "Disruptive Artificial Intelligence and Driverless Self-Driving Cars, and "State-of-the-Art AI Driverless Self-Driving Cars," and "Top Trends in AI Self-Driving Cars," and "AI Innovations and Self-Driving Cars," "Crucial Advances for AI Driverless Cars," "Sociotechnical Insights and AI Driverless Cars," "Pioneering Advances for AI Driverless Cars" and "Leading Edge Trends for AI Driverless Cars," "The Cutting Edge of AI Autonomous Cars" and "The Next Wave of AI Self-Driving Cars" and "Revolutionary Innovations of AI Self-Driving Cars," and "AI Self-Driving Cars Breakthroughs," "Trailblazing Trends for AI Self-Driving Cars," "Ingenious Strides for AI Driverless Cars," and "AI Self-Driving Cars Inventiveness" (they are all available via Amazon). See Appendix A of this herein book to see a listing of the chapters covered in those three books.

For the introduction here to this book, I am going to borrow my introduction from those companion books, since it does a good job of laying out the landscape of self-driving cars and my overall viewpoints on the topic. The remainder of the book is all new material that does not appear in the companion books.

INTRODUCTION TO SELF-DRIVING CARS

This is a book about self-driving cars. Someday in the future, we'll all have self-driving cars and this book will perhaps seem antiquated, but right now, we are at the forefront of the self-driving car wave. Daily news bombards us with flashes of new announcements by one car maker or another and leaves the impression that within the next few weeks or maybe months that the self-driving car will be here. A casual non-technical reader would assume from these news flashes that in fact we must be on the cusp of a true self-driving car.

Here's a real news flash: We are still quite a distance from having a true self-driving car. It is years to go before we get there.

Why is that? Because a true self-driving car is akin to a moonshot. In the same manner that getting us to the moon was an incredible feat, likewise is achieving a true self-driving car. Anybody that suggests or even brashly states that the true self-driving car is nearly here should be viewed with great skepticism. Indeed, you'll see that I often tend to use the word "hogwash" or "crock" when I assess much of the decidedly *fake news* about self-driving cars. Those of us on the inside know that what is often reported to the outside is malarkey. Few of the insiders are willing to say so. I have no such hesitation.

Indeed, I've been writing a popular blog post about self-driving cars and hitting hard on those that try to wave their hands and pretend that we are on the imminent verge of true self-driving cars. For many years, I've been known as the AI Insider. Besides writing about AI, I also develop AI software. I do what I describe. It also gives me insights into what others that are doing AI are really doing versus what it is said they are doing.

Many faithful readers had asked me to pull together my insightful short essays and put them into another book, which you are now holding.

For those of you that have been reading my essays over the years, this collection not only puts them together into one handy package, I also updated the essays and added new material. For those of you that are new to the topic of self-driving cars and AI, I hope you find these essays approachable and informative. I also tend to have a writing style with a bit of a voice, and so you'll see that I am times have a wry sense of humor and poke at conformity.

As a former professor and founder of an AI research lab, I for many years wrote in the formal language of academic writing. I published in referred journals and served as an editor for several AI journals. This writing here is not of the nature, and I have adopted a different and more informal style for these essays. That being said, I also do mention from time-to-time more rigorous material on AI and encourage you all to dig into those deeper and more formal materials if so interested.

I am also an AI practitioner. This means that I write AI software for a living. Currently, I head-up the Cybernetics Self-Driving Car Institute, where we are developing AI software for self-driving cars. I am excited to also report that my son, also a software engineer, heads-up our Cybernetics Self-Driving Car Lab. What I have helped to start, and for which he is an integral part, ultimately he will carry long into the future after I have retired. My daughter, a marketing whiz, also is integral to our efforts as head of our Marketing group. She too will carry forward the legacy now being formulated.

For those of you that are reading this book and have a penchant for writing code, you might consider taking a look at the open source code available for self-driving cars. This is a handy place to start learning how to develop AI for self-driving cars. There are also many new educational courses spring forth. There is a growing body of those wanting to learn about and develop self-driving cars, and a growing body of colleges, labs, and other avenues by which you can learn about self-driving cars.

This book will provide a foundation of aspects that I think will get you ready for those kinds of more advanced training opportunities. If you've already taken those classes, you'll likely find these essays especially interesting as they offer a perspective that I am betting few other instructors or faculty offered to you. These are challenging essays that ask you to think beyond the conventional about self-driving cars.

THE MOTHER OF ALL AI PROJECTS

In June 2017, Apple CEO Tim Cook came out and finally admitted that Apple has been working on a self-driving car. As you'll see in my essays, Apple was enmeshed in secrecy about their self-driving car efforts. We have only been able to read the tea leaves and guess at what Apple has been up to. The notion of an iCar has been floating for quite a while, and self-driving engineers and researchers have been signing tight-lipped Non-Disclosure Agreements (NDA's) to work on projects at Apple that were as shrouded in mystery as any military invasion plans might be.

Tim Cook said something that many others in the Artificial Intelligence (AI) field have been saying, namely, the creation of a self-driving car has got to be the mother of all AI projects. In other words, it is in fact a tremendous moonshot for AI. If a self-driving car can be crafted and the AI works as we hope, it means that we have made incredible strides with AI and that therefore it opens many other worlds of potential breakthrough accomplishments that AI can solve.

Is this hyperbole? Am I just trying to make AI seem like a miracle worker and so provide self-aggrandizing statements for those of us writing the AI software for self-driving cars? No, it is not hyperbole. Developing a true self-driving car is really, really, really hard to do. Let me take a moment to explain why. As a side note, I realize that the Apple CEO is known for at times uttering hyperbole, and he had previously said for example that the year 2012 was "the mother of all years," and he had said that the release of iOS 10 was "the mother of all releases" – all of which does suggest he likes to use the handy "mother of" expression. But, I assure you, in terms of true self-driving cars, he has hit the nail on the head. For sure.

When you think about a moonshot and how we got to the moon, there are some identifiable characteristics and those same aspects can be applied to creating a true self-driving car. You'll notice that I keep putting the word "true" in front of the self-driving car expression. I do so because as per my essay about the various levels of self-driving cars, there are some self-driving cars that are only somewhat of a self-driving car. The somewhat versions are ones that require a human driver to be ready to intervene. In my view, that's not a true self-driving car. A true self-driving car is one that requires no human driver intervention at all. It is a car that can entirely undertake via automation the driving task without any human driver needed. This is the essence of what is known as a Level 5 self-driving car. We are currently at the Level 2 and Level 3 mark, and not yet at Level 5.

Getting to the moon involved aspects such as having big stretch goals, incremental progress, experimentation, innovation, and so on. Let's review how this applied to the moonshot of the bygone era, and how it applies to the self-driving car moonshot of today.

Big Stretch Goal

Trying to take a human and deliver the human to the moon, and bring them back, safely, was an extremely large stretch goal at the time. No one knew whether it could be done. The technology wasn't available yet. The cost was huge. The determination would need to be fierce. Etc. To reach a Level 5 self-driving car is going to be the same. It is a big stretch goal. We can readily get to the Level 3, and we are able to see the Level 4 just up ahead, but a Level 5 is still an unknown as to if it is doable. It should eventually be doable and in the same way that we thought we'd eventually get to the moon, but when it will occur is a different story.

Incremental Progress

Getting to the moon did not happen overnight in one fell swoop. It took years and years of incremental progress to get there. Likewise for self-driving cars. Google has famously been striving to get to the Level 5, and pretty much been willing to forgo dealing with the intervening levels, but most of the other self-driving car makers are doing the incremental route. Let's get a good Level 2 and a somewhat Level 3 going. Then, let's improve the Level 3 and get a somewhat Level 4 going. Then, let's improve the Level 4 and finally arrive at a Level 5. This seems to be the prevalent way that we are going to achieve the true self-driving car.

Experimentation

You likely know that there were various experiments involved in perfecting the approach and technology to get to the moon. As per making incremental progress, we first tried to see if we could get a rocket to go into space and safety return, then put a monkey in there, then with a human, then we went all the way to the moon but didn't land, and finally we arrived at the mission that actually landed on the moon. Self-driving cars are the same way. We are doing simulations of self-driving cars. We do testing of self-driving cars on private land under controlled situations. We do testing of self-driving cars on public roadways, often having to meet regulatory requirements including for example having an engineer or equivalent in the car to take over the controls if needed. And so on. Experiments big and small are needed to figure out what works and what doesn't.

Innovation

There are already some advances in AI that are allowing us to progress toward self-driving cars. We are going to need even more advances. Innovation in all aspects of technology are going to be required to achieve a true self-driving car. By no means do we already have everything in-hand that we need to get there. Expect new inventions and new approaches, new algorithms, etc.

Setbacks

Most of the pundits are avoiding talking about potential setbacks in the progress toward self-driving cars. Getting to the moon involved many setbacks, some of which you never have heard of and were buried at the time so as to not dampen enthusiasm and funding for getting to the moon. A recurring theme in many of my included essays is that there are going to be setbacks as we try to arrive at a true self-driving car. Take a deep breath and be ready. I just hope the setbacks don't completely stop progress. I am sure that it will cause progress to alter in a manner that we've not yet seen in the self-driving car field. I liken the self-driving car of today to the excitement everyone had for Uber when it first got going. Today, we have a different view of Uber and with each passing day there are more regulations to the ride sharing business and more concerns raised. The darling child only stays a darling until finally that child acts up. It will happen the same with self-driving cars.

SELF-DRIVING CARS CHALLENGES

But what exactly makes things so hard to have a true self-driving car, you might be asking. You have seen cruise control for years and years. You've lately seen cars that can do parallel parking. You've seen YouTube videos of Tesla drivers that put their hands out the window as their car zooms along the highway, and seen to therefore be in a self-driving car. Aren't we just needing to put a few more sensors onto a car and then we'll have in-hand a true self-driving car? Nope.

Consider for a moment the nature of the driving task. We don't just let anyone at any age drive a car. Worldwide, most countries won't license a driver until the age of 18, though many do allow a learner's permit at the age of 15 or 16. Some suggest that a younger age would be physically too small to reach the controls of the car. Though this might be the case, we could easily adjust the controls to allow for younger aged and thus smaller stature. It's not their physical size that matters. It's their cognitive development that matters.

To drive a car, you need to be able to reason about the car, what the car can and cannot do. You need to know how to operate the car. You need to know about how other cars on the road drive. You need to know what is allowed in driving such as speed limits and driving within marked lanes. You need to be able to react to situations and be able to avoid getting into accidents. You need to ascertain when to hit your brakes, when to steer clear of a pedestrian, and how to keep from ramming that motorcyclist that just cut you off.

Many of us had taken courses on driving. We studied about driving and took driver training. We had to take a test and pass it to be able to drive. The point being that though most adults take the driving task for granted, and we often "mindlessly" drive our cars, there is a significant amount of cognitive effort that goes into driving a car. After a while, it becomes second nature. You don't especially think about how you drive, you just do it. But, if you watch a novice driver, say a teenager learning to drive, you suddenly realize that there is a lot more complexity to it than we seem to realize.

Furthermore, driving is a very serious task. I recall when my daughter and son first learned to drive. They are both very conscientious people. They wanted to make sure that whatever they did, they did well, and that they did not harm anyone. Every day, when you get into a car, it is probably around 4,000 pounds of hefty metal and plastics (about two tons), and it is a lethal weapon. Think about it. You drive down the street in an object that weighs two tons and with the engine it can accelerate and ram into anything you want to hit. The damage a car can inflict is very scary. Both my children were surprised that they were being given the right to maneuver this monster of a beast that could cause tremendous harm entirely by merely letting go of the steering wheel for a moment or taking your eyes off the road.

In fact, in the United States alone there are about 30,000 deaths per year by auto accidents, which is around 100 per day. Given that there are about 263 million cars in the United States, I am actually more amazed that the number of fatalities is not a lot higher. During my morning commute, I look at all the thousands of cars on the freeway around me, and I think that if all of them decided to go zombie and drive in a crazy maniac way, there would be many people dead. Somehow, incredibly, each day, most people drive relatively safely. To me, that's a miracle right there. Getting millions and millions of people to be safe and sane when behind the wheel of a two ton mobile object, it's a feat that we as a society should admire with pride.

So, hopefully you are in agreement that the driving task requires a great deal of cognition. You don't' need to be especially smart to drive a car, and we've done quite a bit to make car driving viable for even the average dolt. There isn't an IQ test that you need to take to drive a car. If you can read and write, and pass a test, you pretty much can legally drive a car. There are of course some that drive a car and are not legally permitted to do so, plus there are private areas such as farms where drivers are young, but for public roadways in the United States, you can be generally of average intelligence (or less) and be able to legally drive.

This though makes it seem like the cognitive effort must not be much. If the cognitive effort was truly hard, wouldn't we only have Einstein's that could drive a car? We have made sure to keep the driving task as simple as we can, by making the controls easy and relatively standardized, and by having roads that are relatively standardized, and so on. It is as though Disneyland has put their Autopia into the real-world, by us all as a society agreeing that roads will be a certain way, and we'll all abide by the various rules of driving.

A modest cognitive task by a human is still something that stymies AI. You certainly know that AI has been able to beat chess players and be good at other kinds of games. This type of narrow cognition is not what car driving is about. Car driving is much wider. It requires knowledge about the world, which a chess playing AI system does not need to know. The cognitive aspects of driving are on the one hand seemingly simple, but at the same time require layer upon layer of knowledge about cars, people, roads, rules, and a myriad of other "common sense" aspects. We don't have any AI systems today that have that same kind of breadth and depth of awareness and knowledge.

As revealed in my essays, the self-driving car of today is using trickery to do particular tasks. It is all very narrow in operation. Plus, it currently assumes that a human driver is ready to intervene. It is like a child that we have taught to stack blocks, but we are needed to be right there in case the child stacks them too high and they begin to fall over. AI of today is brittle, it is narrow, and it does not approach the cognitive abilities of humans. This is why the true self-driving car is somewhere out in the future.

Another aspect to the driving task is that it is not solely a mind exercise. You do need to use your senses to drive. You use your eyes a vision sensors to see the road ahead. You vision capability is like a streaming video, which your brain needs to continually analyze as you drive. Where is the road? Is there a pedestrian in the way? Is there another car ahead of you? Your senses are relying a flood of info to your brain. Self-driving cars are trying to do the same, by using cameras, radar, ultrasound, and lasers. This is an attempt at mimicking how humans have senses and sensory apparatus.

Thus, the driving task is mental and physical. You use your senses, you use your arms and legs to manipulate the controls of the car, and you use your brain to assess the sensory info and direct your limbs to act upon the controls of the car. This all happens instantly. If you've ever perhaps gotten something in your eye and only had one eye available to drive with, you suddenly realize how dependent upon vision you are. If you have a broken foot with a cast, you suddenly realize how hard it is to control the brake pedal and the accelerator. If you've taken medication and your brain is maybe sluggish, you suddenly realize how much mental strain is required to drive a car.

An AI system that plays chess only needs to be focused on playing chess. The physical aspects aren't important because usually a human moves the chess pieces or the chessboard is shown on an electronic display. Using AI for a more life-and-death task such as analyzing MRI images of patients, this again does not require physical capabilities and instead is done by examining images of bits.

Driving a car is a true life-and-death task. It is a use of AI that can easily and at any moment produce death. For those colleagues of mine that are developing this AI, as am I, we need to keep in mind the somber aspects of this. We are producing software that will have in its virtual hands the lives of the occupants of the car, and the lives of those in other nearby cars, and the lives of nearby pedestrians, etc. Chess is not usually a life-or-death matter.

Driving is all around us. Cars are everywhere. Most of today's AI applications involve only a small number of people. Or, they are behind the scenes and we as humans have other recourse if the AI messes up. AI that is driving a car at 80 miles per hour on a highway had better not mess up. The consequences are grave. Multiply this by the number of cars, if we could put magically self-driving into every car in the USA, we'd have AI running in the 263 million cars. That's a lot of AI spread around. This is AI on a massive scale that we are not doing today and that offers both promise and potential peril.

There are some that want AI for self-driving cars because they envision a world without any car accidents. They envision a world in which there is no car congestion and all cars cooperate with each other. These are wonderful utopian visions.

They are also very misleading. The adoption of self-driving cars is going to be incremental and not overnight. We cannot economically just junk all existing cars. Nor are we going to be able to affordably retrofit existing cars. It is more likely that self-driving cars will be built into new cars and that over many years of gradual replacement of existing cars that we'll see the mix of self-driving cars become substantial in the real-world.

In these essays, I have tried to offer technological insights without being overly technical in my description, and also blended the business, societal, and economic aspects too. Technologists need to consider the non-technological impacts of what they do. Non-technologists should be aware of what is being developed.

We all need to work together to collectively be prepared for the enormous disruption and transformative aspects of true self-driving cars. We all need to be involved in this mother of all AI projects.

WHAT THIS BOOK PROVIDES

What does this book provide to you? It introduces many of the key elements about self-driving cars and does so with an AI based perspective. I weave together technical and non-technical aspects, readily going from being concerned about the cognitive capabilities of the driving task and how the technology is embodying this into self-driving cars, and in the next breath I discuss the societal and economic aspects.

They are all intertwined because that's the way reality is. You cannot separate out the technology per se, and instead must consider it within the milieu of what is being invented and innovated, and do so with a mindset towards the contemporary mores and culture that shape what we are doing and what we hope to do.

WHY THIS BOOK

I wrote this book to try and bring to the public view many aspects about self-driving cars that nobody seems to be discussing.

For business leaders that are either involved in making self-driving cars or that are going to leverage self-driving cars, I hope that this book will enlighten you as to the risks involved and ways in which you should be strategizing about how to deal with those risks.

For entrepreneurs, startups and other businesses that want to enter into the self-driving car market that is emerging, I hope this book sparks your interest in doing so, and provides some sense of what might be prudent to pursue.

For researchers that study self-driving cars, I hope this book spurs your interest in the risks and safety issues of self-driving cars, and also nudges you toward conducting research on those aspects.

For students in computer science or related disciplines, I hope this book will provide you with interesting and new ideas and material, for which you might conduct research or provide some career direction insights for you.

For AI companies and high-tech companies pursuing self-driving cars, this book will hopefully broaden your view beyond just the mere coding and development needed to make self-driving cars.

For all readers, I hope that you will find the material in this book to be stimulating. Some of it will be repetitive of things you already know. But I am pretty sure that you'll also find various eureka moments whereby you'll discover a new technique or approach that you had not earlier thought of. I am also betting that there will be material that forces you to rethink some of your current practices.

I am not saying you will suddenly have an epiphany and change what you are doing. I do think though that you will reconsider or perhaps revisit what you are doing.

For anyone choosing to use this book for teaching purposes, please take a look at my suggestions for doing so, as described in the Appendix. I have found the material handy in courses that I have taught, and likewise other faculty have told me that they have found the material handy, in some cases as extended readings and in other instances as a core part of their course (depending on the nature of the class).

In my writing for this book, I have tried carefully to blend both the practitioner and the academic styles of writing. It is not as dense as is typical academic journal writing, but at the same time offers depth by going into the nuances and trade-offs of various practices.

The word "deep" is in vogue today, meaning getting deeply into a subject or topic, and so is the word "unpack" which means to tease out the underlying aspects of a subject or topic. I have sought to offer material that addresses an issue or topic by going relatively deeply into it and make sure that it is well unpacked.

Finally, in any book about AI, it is difficult to use our everyday words without having some of them be misinterpreted. Specifically, it is easy to anthropomorphize AI. When I say that an AI system "knows" something, I do not want you to construe that the AI system has sentience and "knows" in the same way that humans do. They aren't that way, as yet. I have tried to use quotes around such words from time-to-time to emphasize that the words I am using should not be misinterpreted to ascribe true human intelligence to the AI systems that we know of today. If I used quotes around all such words, the book would be very difficult to read, and so I am doing so judiciously. Please keep that in mind as you read the material, thanks.

COMPANION BOOKS

If you find this material of interest, you might enjoy these too:

1. **"Introduction to Driverless Self-Driving Cars"** by Dr. Lance Eliot

2. **"Innovation and Thought Leadership on Self-Driving Driverless Cars"** by Dr. Lance Eliot

3. **"Advances in AI and Autonomous Vehicles: Cybernetic Self-Driving Cars"** by Dr. Lance Eliot

4. **"Self-Driving Cars: The Mother of All AI Projects"** by Dr. Lance Eliot

5. **"New Advances in AI Autonomous Driverless Self-Driving Cars"** by Dr. Lance Eliot

6. **"Autonomous Vehicle Driverless Self-Driving Cars and Artificial Intelligence"** by Dr. Lance Eliot and Michael B. Eliot

7. **"Transformative Artificial Intelligence Driverless Self-Driving Cars"** by Dr. Lance Eliot

8. **"Disruptive Artificial Intelligence and Driverless Self-Driving Cars"** by Dr. Lance Eliot

9. "State-of-the-Art AI Driverless Self-Driving Cars" by Dr. Lance Eliot

10. **"Top Trends in AI Self-Driving Cars"** by Dr. Lance Eliot

11. **"AI Innovations and Self-Driving Cars"** by Dr. Lance Eliot

12. **"Crucial Advances for AI Driverless Cars"** by Dr. Lance Eliot

13. **"Sociotechnical Insights and AI Driverless Cars"** by Dr. Lance Eliot.

14. **"Pioneering Advances for AI Driverless Cars"** by Dr. Lance Eliot

15. **"Leading Edge Trends for AI Driverless Cars"** by Dr. Lance Eliot

16. **"The Cutting Edge of AI Autonomous Cars"** by Dr. Lance Eliot

17. **"The Next Wave of AI Self-Driving Cars"** by Dr. Lance Eliot

18. **"Revolutionary Innovations of AI Driverless Cars"** by Dr. Lance Eliot

19. **"AI Self-Driving Cars Breakthroughs"** by Dr. Lance Eliot

20. **"Trailblazing Trends for AI Self-Driving Cars"** by Dr. Lance Eliot

21. **"Ingenious Strides for AI Driverless Cars"** by Dr. Lance Eliot

22. **"AI Self-Driving Cars Inventiveness"** by Dr. Lance Eliot

All of the above books are available on Amazon and at other major global booksellers.

CHAPTER 1

ELIOT FRAMEWORK FOR AI SELF-DRIVING CARS

CHAPTER 1

ELIOT FRAMEWORK FOR AI SELF-DRIVING CARS

This chapter is a core foundational aspect for understanding AI self-driving cars and I have used this same chapter in several of my other books to introduce the reader to essential elements of this field. Once you've read this chapter, you'll be prepared to read the rest of the material since the foundational essence of the components of autonomous AI driverless self-driving cars will have been established for you.

———————

When I give presentations about self-driving cars and teach classes on the topic, I have found it helpful to provide a framework around which the various key elements of self-driving cars can be understood and organized (see diagram at the end of this chapter). The framework needs to be simple enough to convey the overarching elements, but at the same time not so simple that it belies the true complexity of self-driving cars. As such, I am going to describe the framework here and try to offer in a thousand words (or more!) what the framework diagram itself intends to portray.

The core elements on the diagram are numbered for ease of reference. The numbering does not suggest any kind of prioritization of the elements. Each element is crucial. Each element has a purpose, and otherwise would not be included in the framework. For some self-driving cars, a particular element might be more important or somehow distinguished in comparison to other self-driving cars.

You could even use the framework to rate a particular self-driving car, doing so by gauging how well it performs in each of the elements of the framework. I will describe each of the elements, one at a time. After doing so, I'll discuss aspects that illustrate how the elements interact and perform during the overall effort of a self-driving car.

At the Cybernetic Self-Driving Car Institute, we use the framework to keep track of what we are working on, and how we are developing software that fills in what is needed to achieve Level 5 self-driving cars.

D-01: Sensor Capture

Let's start with the one element that often gets the most attention in the press about self-driving cars, namely, the sensory devices for a self-driving car.

On the framework, the box labeled as D-01 indicates "Sensor Capture" and refers to the processes of the self-driving car that involve collecting data from the myriad of sensors that are used for a self-driving car. The types of devices typically involved are listed, such as the use of mono cameras, stereo cameras, LIDAR devices, radar systems, ultrasonic devices, GPS, IMU, and so on.

These devices are tasked with obtaining data about the status of the self-driving car and the world around it. Some of the devices are continually providing updates, while others of the devices await an indication by the self-driving car that the device is supposed to collect data. The data might be first transformed in some fashion by the device itself, or it might instead be fed directly into the sensor capture as raw data. At that point, it might be up to the sensor capture processes to do transformations on the data. This all varies depending upon the nature of the devices being used and how the devices were designed and developed.

D-02: Sensor Fusion

Imagine that your eyeballs receive visual images, your nose receives odors, your ears receive sounds, and in essence each of your distinct sensory devices is getting some form of input. The input befits the nature of the device. Likewise, for a self-driving car, the cameras provide visual images, the radar returns radar reflections, and so on.

Each device provides the data as befits what the device does.

At some point, using the analogy to humans, you need to merge together what your eyes see, what your nose smells, what your ears hear, and piece it all together into a larger sense of what the world is all about and what is happening around you. Sensor fusion is the action of taking the singular aspects from each of the devices and putting them together into a larger puzzle.

Sensor fusion is a tough task. There are some devices that might not be working at the time of the sensor capture. Or, there might some devices that are unable to report well what they have detected. Again, using a human analogy, suppose you are in a dark room and so your eyes cannot see much. At that point, you might need to rely more so on your ears and what you hear. The same is true for a self-driving car. If the cameras are obscured due to snow and sleet, it might be that the radar can provide a greater indication of what the external conditions consist of.

In the case of a self-driving car, there can be a plethora of such sensory devices. Each is reporting what it can. Each might have its difficulties. Each might have its limitations, such as how far ahead it can detect an object. All of these limitations need to be considered during the sensor fusion task.

D-03: Virtual World Model

For humans, we presumably keep in our minds a model of the world around us when we are driving a car. In your mind, you know that the car is going at say 60 miles per hour and that you are on a freeway. You have a model in your mind that your car is surrounded by other cars, and that there are lanes to the freeway. Your model is not only based on what you can see, hear, etc., but also what you know about the nature of the world. You know that at any moment that car ahead of you can smash on its brakes, or the car behind you can ram into your car, or that the truck in the next lane might swerve into your lane.

The AI of the self-driving car needs to have a virtual world model, which it then keeps updated with whatever it is receiving from the sensor fusion, which received its input from the sensor capture and the sensory devices.

D-04: System Action Plan

By having a virtual world model, the AI of the self-driving car is able to keep track of where the car is and what is happening around the car. In addition, the AI needs to determine what to do next. Should the self-driving car hit its brakes? Should the self-driving car stay in its lane or swerve into the lane to the left? Should the self-driving car accelerate or slow down?

A system action plan needs to be prepared by the AI of the self-driving car. The action plan specifies what actions should be taken. The actions need to pertain to the status of the virtual world model. Plus, the actions need to be realizable.

This realizability means that the AI cannot just assert that the self-driving car should suddenly sprout wings and fly. Instead, the AI must be bound by whatever the self-driving car can actually do, such as coming to a halt in a distance of X feet at a speed of Y miles per hour, rather than perhaps asserting that the self-driving car come to a halt in 0 feet as though it could instantaneously come to a stop while it is in motion.

D-05: Controls Activation

The system action plan is implemented by activating the controls of the car to act according to what the plan stipulates. This might mean that the accelerator control is commanded to increase the speed of the car. Or, the steering control is commanded to turn the steering wheel 30 degrees to the left or right.

One question arises as to whether or not the controls respond as they are commanded to do. In other words, suppose the AI has commanded the accelerator to increase, but for some reason it does not do so. Or, maybe it tries to do so, but the speed of the car does not increase. The controls activation feeds back into the virtual world model, and simultaneously the virtual world model is getting updated from the sensors, the sensor capture, and the sensor fusion. This allows the AI to ascertain what has taken place as a result of the controls being commanded to take some kind of action.

By the way, please keep in mind that though the diagram seems to have a linear progression to it, the reality is that these are all aspects of the self-driving car that are happening in parallel and simultaneously. The sensors are capturing data, meanwhile the sensor fusion is taking place, meanwhile the virtual model is being updated, meanwhile the system action plan is being formulated and reformulated, meanwhile the controls are being activated.

This is the same as a human being that is driving a car. They are eyeballing the road, meanwhile they are fusing in their mind the sights, sounds, etc., meanwhile their mind is updating their model of the world around them, meanwhile they are formulating an action plan of what to do, and meanwhile they are pushing their foot onto the pedals and steering the car. In the normal course of driving a car, you are doing all of these at once. I mention this so that when you look at the diagram, you will think of the boxes as processes that are all happening at the same time, and not as though only one happens and then the next.

They are shown diagrammatically in a simplistic manner to help comprehend what is taking place. You though should also realize that they are working in parallel and simultaneous with each other. This is a tough aspect in that the inter-element communications involve latency and other aspects that must be taken into account. There can be delays in one element updating and then sharing its latest status with other elements.

D-06: Automobile & CAN

Contemporary cars use various automotive electronics and a Controller Area Network (CAN) to serve as the components that underlie the driving aspects of a car. There are Electronic Control Units (ECU's) which control subsystems of the car, such as the engine, the brakes, the doors, the windows, and so on.

The elements D-01, D-02, D-03, D-04, D-05 are layered on top of the D-06, and must be aware of the nature of what the D-06 is able to do and not do.

D-07: In-Car Commands

Humans are going to be occupants in self-driving cars. In a Level 5 self-driving car, there must be some form of communication that takes place between the humans and the self-driving car. For example, I go into a self-driving car and tell it that I want to be driven over to Disneyland, and along the way I want to stop at In-and-Out Burger. The self-driving car now parses what I've said and tries to then establish a means to carry out my wishes.

In-car commands can happen at any time during a driving journey. Though my example was about an in-car command when I first got into my self-driving car, it could be that while the self-driving car is carrying out the journey that I change my mind. Perhaps after getting stuck in traffic, I tell the self-driving car to forget about getting the burgers and just head straight over to the theme park. The self-driving car needs to be alert to in-car commands throughout the journey.

D-08: V2X Communications

We will ultimately have self-driving cars communicating with each other, doing so via V2V (Vehicle-to-Vehicle) communications. We will also have self-driving cars that communicate with the roadways and other aspects of the transportation infrastructure, doing so via V2I (Vehicle-to-Infrastructure).

The variety of ways in which a self-driving car will be communicating with other cars and infrastructure is being called V2X, whereby the letter X means whatever else we identify as something that a car should or would want to communicate with. The V2X communications will be taking place simultaneous with everything else on the diagram, and those other elements will need to incorporate whatever it gleans from those V2X communications.

D-09: Deep Learning

The use of Deep Learning permeates all other aspects of the self-driving car. The AI of the self-driving car will be using deep learning to do a better job at the systems action plan, and at the controls activation, and at the sensor fusion, and so on.

Currently, the use of artificial neural networks is the most prevalent form of deep learning. Based on large swaths of data, the neural networks attempt to "learn" from the data and therefore direct the efforts of the self-driving car accordingly.

D-10: Tactical AI

Tactical AI is the element of dealing with the moment-to-moment driving of the self-driving car. Is the self-driving car staying in its lane of the freeway? Is the car responding appropriately to the controls commands? Are the sensory devices working?

For human drivers, the tactical equivalent can be seen when you watch a novice driver such as a teenager that is first driving. They are focused on the mechanics of the driving task, keeping their eye on the road while also trying to properly control the car.

D-11: Strategic AI

The Strategic AI aspects of a self-driving car are dealing with the larger picture of what the self-driving car is trying to do. If I had asked that the self-driving car take me to Disneyland, there is an overall journey map that needs to be kept and maintained.

There is an interaction between the Strategic AI and the Tactical AI. The Strategic AI is wanting to keep on the mission of the driving, while the Tactical AI is focused on the particulars underway in the driving effort. If the Tactical AI seems to wander away from the overarching mission, the Strategic AI wants to see why and get things back on track. If the Tactical AI realizes that there is something amiss on the self-driving car, it needs to alert the Strategic AI accordingly and have an adjustment to the overarching mission that is underway.

D-12: Self-Aware AI

Very few of the self-driving cars being developed are including a Self-Aware AI element, which we at the Cybernetic Self-Driving Car Institute believe is crucial to Level 5 self-driving cars.

The Self-Aware AI element is intended to watch over itself, in the sense that the AI is making sure that the AI is working as intended. Suppose you had a human driving a car, and they were starting to drive erratically. Hopefully, their own self-awareness would make them realize they themselves are driving poorly, such as perhaps starting to fall asleep after having been driving for hours on end. If you had a passenger in the car, they might be able to alert the driver if the driver is starting to do something amiss. This is exactly what the Self-Aware

AI element tries to do, it becomes the overseer of the AI, and tries to detect when the AI has become faulty or confused, and then find ways to overcome the issue.

D-13: Economic

The economic aspects of a self-driving car are not per se a technology aspect of a self-driving car, but the economics do indeed impact the nature of a self-driving car. For example, the cost of outfitting a self-driving car with every kind of possible sensory device is prohibitive, and so choices need to be made about which devices are used. And, for those sensory devices chosen, whether they would have a full set of features or a more limited set of features.

We are going to have self-driving cars that are at the low-end of a consumer cost point, and others at the high-end of a consumer cost point. You cannot expect that the self-driving car at the low-end is going to be as robust as the one at the high-end. I realize that many of the self-driving car pundits are acting as though all self-driving cars will be the same, but they won't be. Just like anything else, we are going to have self-driving cars that have a range of capabilities. Some will be better than others. Some will be safer than others. This is the way of the real-world, and so we need to be thinking about the economics aspects when considering the nature of self-driving cars.

D-14: Societal

This component encompasses the societal aspects of AI which also impacts the technology of self-driving cars. For example, the famous Trolley Problem involves what choices should a self-driving car make when faced with life-and-death matters. If the self-driving car is about to either hit a child standing in the roadway, or instead ram into a tree at the side of the road and possibly kill the humans in the self-driving car, which choice should be made?

We need to keep in mind the societal aspects will underlie the AI of the self-driving car. Whether we are aware of it explicitly or not, the AI will have embedded into it various societal assumptions.

D-15: Innovation

I included the notion of innovation into the framework because we can anticipate that whatever a self-driving car consists of, it will continue to be innovated over time. The self-driving cars coming out in the next several years will undoubtedly be different and less innovative than the versions that come out in ten years hence, and so on.

Framework Overall

For those of you that want to learn about self-driving cars, you can potentially pick a particular element and become specialized in that aspect. Some engineers are focusing on the sensory devices. Some engineers focus on the controls activation. And so on. There are specialties in each of the elements.

Researchers are likewise specializing in various aspects. For example, there are researchers that are using Deep Learning to see how best it can be used for sensor fusion. There are other researchers that are using Deep Learning to derive good System Action Plans. Some are studying how to develop AI for the Strategic aspects of the driving task, while others are focused on the Tactical aspects.

A well-prepared all-around software developer that is involved in self-driving cars should be familiar with all of the elements, at least to the degree that they know what each element does. This is important since whatever piece of the pie that the software developer works on, they need to be knowledgeable about what the other elements are doing.

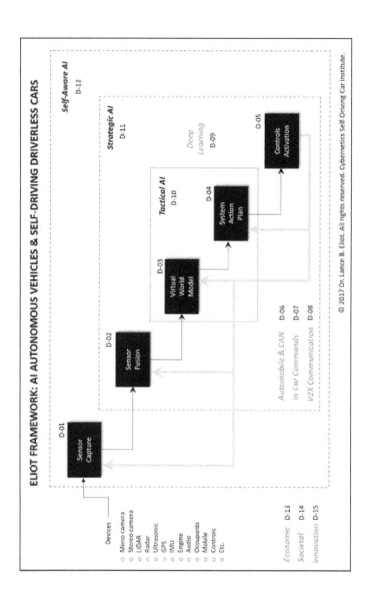

ELIOT FRAMEWORK: AI AUTONOMOUS VEHICLES & SELF-DRIVING DRIVERLESS CARS

© 2017 Dr. Lance B. Eliot. All rights reserved. Cybernetics Self-Driving Car Institute.

CHAPTER 2

CRUMBLING INFRASTRUCTURE AND AI SELF-DRIVING CARS

CHAPTER 2

CRUMBLING INFRASTRUCTURE AND AI SELF-DRIVING CARS

I should sue! That's what my friends told me to do. They were looking at the damage done to the right fender and front right tire of my car. I had been driving innocently down a street in downtown Los Angeles and encountered a whopper of a pothole. I was doing the legal speed limit and was not driving recklessly. When I turned a corner, an unexpected pothole loomed just after making the turn, and the right side of my car was doomed to enter into the gaping asphalt gash.

My guess is that I was going relatively slowly as I made the turn and it seemed to me that such a low speed would have made hitting the pothole a non-issue. Nonetheless, there was a loud bang and scraping sound when I hit the pothole. I quickly pulled over to the side of the road to do a quick visual inspection of my car. The fender was scrapped and slightly bent. The tire appeared to be intact but had a strange bulbous-like protrusion now at the surface of the rubber.

Certainly, I was not the first person to find myself having become a victim of this particular pothole. This specific street was popular since it led you to the on-ramp for the Harbor Freeway. Typically, each day, downtown L.A. office workers would go this way in the evening after work to get onto the freeway and make their way home. I'd bet that tons of drivers had hit that pothole. Maybe I should launch a class action lawsuit rather than suing solely on my own behalf!

Potholes like this monster tend to get worse over time. More and more cars fall into it or ram it or roll over it, all of which causes the hole to widen and deepen. Now I'm not saying that this was one of those huge abyss-like monstrosities that seem to swallow-up entire cars. Admittedly, this pothole was still in its infancy. But, however you want to characterize it, the hole was relatively lethal and had already taken a chomp out of my car.

It was quite unsettling when I hit the pothole. It made me wonder afterwards if other driver's might lose control of their car or become so startled that they might drive wildly after having struck the pothole. I watched for a few moments to see what other drivers did, and by-and-large most of them seemed to take the banging and bumping of hitting the pothole in stride. They probably had experienced this pothole before, or perhaps have encountered so many potholes throughout the Southern California area that they had become numb to hitting them.

There were a few drivers that struck the pothole and definitely appeared to momentarily nearly lose control of their car. They swerved toward the curb that was just a few feet from the hole. I suppose it was possible that if a pedestrian happened to be standing at that exact spot on the sidewalk, perhaps right at the curb, maybe waiting to get a ridesharing lift, they could have been endangered.

It would have to be some driver that really got a shock from plastering into the pothole, though this is not as remote a chance as you might think. There are lots of Los Angeles drivers that I'd dare say should probably not have a driver's license as they seem to drive without any due care or drive like a frightened mouse that goes a kilter at the slightest afront. A novice teenage driver just learning to drive might be taken aback by hitting the hole and perhaps lose control of their car. Besides cars, I also considered the impact of a motorcyclist hitting the pothole and the idea made me shudder.

Some of you might be thinking that I was not properly paying attention to the road and that if I had been more alert that I would have seen the pothole before striking it. I would like to argue that point with you. I went back to the corner and drove the turn again, wanting to see if it was feasible to see the pothole before making the turn. I suppose that I was trying to amass evidence for suing, or at least to be able to explain to my friends why I "stupidly" struck a gap pothole.

At the turn, there were too many other objects nearby to be able to clearly see the roadway beyond the corner. There was a fire hydrant near to the corner. There was a pedestrian stand. There was a posted sign about when you could park on that street. There was a street sign indicating the name of the street. All in all, even if you knew to look for the pothole, it was well obscured by the other objects at the corner.

Upon making the turn, you would only have a split second to see the pothole. I estimated that you would need to be crawling at the lowest possible speed of a car to have any amount of time to first notice the pothole and then take an evasive maneuver. Let's also keep in mind that if you did magically see the pothole in time to make an evasive maneuver, what maneuver would you make?

If you tried to swing wide to the left around the pothole, there was a danger of striking another car coming down the street. If going left was unwise, going to the right was equally unwise or worse. There was insufficient room to try and go to the right of the pothole, which you'd end-up having to drive up onto the curb. You could try to weave directly over the pothole, putting your right tire just to the right of the pothole, making sure to keep the tire in the gutter next to the curb and not go up over the curb. This was a rather finesse-like approach and would have taken some advanced preparations to get to just the correct position moments before coming upon the hole.

Generally, I would say that the "safest" approach was to go ahead and bite-the-bullet and hit the pothole, assuming that you were not forewarned about its presence. Hitting the pothole and making sure to keep control of your car seemed a less risky approach than the other alternatives. Trying to hit the brakes just as you encountered the pothole was another possibility, but I'd bet that a car behind you that was also making the same turn would have been likely to rear-end your car.

I realize you might say that would be their fault, and I get that notion, regardless though I'd rather take the chance of harming my suspension or my tire versus getting struck by another car from behind and possibly suffering whiplash.

For those of you in the hyper-digital age, you might be yelling at me right now and clamoring that I ought to be using a traffic app on my smartphone that might have warned me about the pothole. Indeed, there are a number of traffic or roadway related apps that allow a crowdsourcing approach to keeping track of the deteriorating roadway infrastructure. People using the app can mark spots that contains potholes and other roadway difficulties. Other people using the app can then be forewarned.

There are some apps that also allow the posted item to be transmitted to the local roadway repair crews. Of course, it isn't as though a roadway repair crew is going to instantaneously appear and fix the hole or other roadway matter. The odds are that they have hundreds or maybe thousands of these kinds of reported roadway issues. They need to prioritize which ones they work on. It takes time for the crew to come out and make the repair. Presumably, the worse of the roadway blemishes that present the highest risk to drivers and pedestrians are getting the higher priority over the other bothersome but not "killer" kinds of roadway problems.

One concern expressed by those that study our crumbling roadway infrastructure is that we seem to be mired in a continual mode of quick repair. This fix-and-forget kind of approach is belied by the fact that often times a repair is made that lasts only a short time. For the pothole at the corner, suppose a repair crew slops in some fresh asphalt. It might fill-in the hole for a brief period of time. Meanwhile, cars continue to roll over the patch and the pothole will be potentially reborn. Sure enough, the pothole might become a monster again, and the cycle of coming to do another quick-fix will repeat itself.

The American Society of Civil Engineers recently published a report that says there are around 57% of the roads in Los Angeles that can be rated at a poor condition. By poor condition, they are asserting that those roads are in significant deterioration, are well-below roadway standards, and have a strong risk of overall failure. In my daily one to two-hour commute here in Southern California, I'd wholeheartedly agree that at least seemingly half of the roads are in bad shape here. Maybe more. Maybe a lot more.

Those of you that aren't here in California are probably not especially sympathetic to our roadway plight in that you likely have something going on where you live that has a similar gloomy roadway dilemma, perhaps even worse than our roads. Here's a big number for you: $4.6 trillion dollars. That's how much the American Society of Civil Engineers estimates is the cumulative price needed to make our U.S. transportation infrastructure into something of an above average grade (right now, they say that the U.S. is maybe a D+).

My story about the pothole is really a microcosm of our overall roadway infrastructure. We have lots and lots of infrastructure that is crumbling around us. We depend upon the infrastructure to make our way to work and for going to the store and for living our lives. The infrastructure is decaying and wearing out. Attempts at quick fixes are only momentarily keeping things intact. One might claim that those quick fixes end-up masking the overarching problems and we are therefore deluding ourselves by making the quick fixes.

Our economy depends upon our ability to drive on the roads. One could say that our society depends on our ability to drive on the roads. Our elaborate and crisscrossing roadway infrastructure is the essence of how we live.

It is easy to take it for granted.

When I tell people that we need to do something about our roads, I usually get a kind of yawn and am told that we just need to all stop whining (though, once they themselves have hit a pothole, and felt the "pain" of our worsening roads, they suddenly become converts to doing something about the infrastructure!). When I tell people about the nearly $5 trillion dollars needed to invest in our infrastructure to keep it going and hopefully bolster it, the number is so astronomical that most people cannot fathom how much money that is.

What does this have to do with AI self-driving cars?

At the Cybernetic AI Self-Driving Car Institute, we are developing AI software for self-driving cars. One aspect involves making sure that the AI can handle driving on rough roads and contend with our deteriorating roadway infrastructure.

Allow me to elaborate.

I'd like to first clarify and introduce the notion that there are varying levels of AI self-driving cars. The topmost level is considered Level 5. A Level 5 self-driving car is one that is being driven by the AI and there is no human driver involved. For the design of Level 5 self-driving cars, the auto makers are even removing the gas pedal, brake pedal, and steering wheel, since those are contraptions used by human drivers. The Level 5 self-driving car is not being driven by a human and nor is there an expectation that a human driver will be present in the self-driving car. It's all on the shoulders of the AI to drive the car.

For self-driving cars less than a Level 5, there must be a human driver present in the car. The human driver is currently considered the responsible party for the acts of the car. The AI and the human driver are co-sharing the driving task. In spite of this co-sharing, the human is supposed to remain fully immersed into the driving task and be ready at all times to perform the driving task. I've repeatedly warned about the dangers of this co-sharing arrangement and predicted it will produce many untoward results.

Let's focus herein on the true Level 5 self-driving car. Much of the comments apply to the less than Level 5 self-driving cars too, but the fully autonomous AI self-driving car will receive the most attention in this discussion.

Here's the usual steps involved in the AI driving task:

- Sensor data collection and interpretation
- Sensor fusion
- Virtual world model updating
- AI action planning
- Car controls command issuance

Another key aspect of AI self-driving cars is that they will be driving on our roadways in the midst of human driven cars too. There are some pundits of AI self-driving cars that continually refer to a utopian world in which there are only AI self-driving cars on the public roads. Currently there are about 250+ million conventional cars in the United States alone, and those cars are not going to magically disappear or become true Level 5 AI self-driving cars overnight.

Indeed, the use of human driven cars will last for many years, likely many decades, and the advent of AI self-driving cars will occur while there are still human driven cars on the roads. This is a crucial point since this means that the AI of self-driving cars needs to be able to contend with not just other AI self-driving cars, but also contend with human driven cars. It is easy to envision a simplistic and rather unrealistic world in which all AI self-driving cars are politely interacting with each other and being civil about roadway interactions. That's not what is going to be happening for the foreseeable future. AI self-driving cars and human driven cars will need to be able to cope with each other.

Let's consider what kind of impact this crumbling infrastructure situation might have on AI self-driving cars, along with pondering the future of the infrastructure as framed in light of the hopeful and likely advent of AI self-driving cars.

We'll start with the assumption that the roads will continue for the foreseeable future to deteriorate and it will be a sad and unavoidable fact of life.

As such, what should AI developers be doing in terms of the AI for self-driving cars? Some AI developers tell me that there's nothing special they need to do. The road is the road. Good or bad, there's presumably no need to care. Just focus on having the AI be able to drive a car and that's sufficient, in their book.

I tend to disagree with their head-in-the-sand approach. We believe that the AI ought to be specially prepared for a likely lousy infrastructure that contains roadway potholes, pits, cracks, debris, and for which the painted lines on the roads will be faded or disappear, and that street signs might be obscured or missing, etc. These are all the potential and inevitable consequences if there is not something Herculean done to improve the infrastructure.

One aspect that catches the attention of the AI developers that don't seem to believe in caring about the untoward infrastructure involves my mentioning the faded or disappearance of lane markers and lane lines. This gets those AI developers to suddenly pay attention. The reason for their attention is that many of them are using the now-classic navigation technique of watching for lane markers and lane lines to know where the AI is supposed to position the self-driving car.

The AI system uses the camera sensors to try and detect where those lane markers and lane lines are. Then, once so detected, the AI guides the controls of the self-driving car to stay within those lines when traveling in a lane, and also for purposes of changing lanes. It is essential that this AI approach must have available relatively obvious and clear-cut lane markings. Without the lane markings, the AI system is pretty much unable to discern where a lane is and where to keep the self-driving car while moving along on the roads.

Human drivers of course also depend upon the lane markers and lane lines, but they are also able to handle a great deal of ambiguity when the lane indications are slim or intermittent. Us humans seem to be able to mentally gauge where a lane might or must be, even when the lane itself does not standout or otherwise has evaporated in terms of a marked path. That's how good us humans are. Sure, I realize that some humans do get confused in such cases, and they might weave or wander into someone else's pretend lane, but by-and-large most capable human drivers can handle this vagueness when it occurs.

So, the point is that the traditional AI technique of relying on apparent lane markings and lane lines is likely to get undermined as the roadways worsen. It is crucial to bump-up the AI to be more sophisticated in ascertaining lane positioning. If we don't boost the AI for this, the vaunted hope of having less fatalities due to the advent of AI self-driving cars will be called more so into question.

Another aspect about the AI system is that it needs to be using all of its capabilities to try and detect roadway issues and obstacles, which will be even more so crucial as the crumbling infrastructure continues to degrade.

Let's use my pothole example. As mentioned, I was unable to detect the pothole prior to making the right turn at the corner of the downtown street. Could the AI have done a better job?

I'm not so sure it could have in this circumstance since the visual images coming into the cameras of the self-driving car would not have readily revealed the pothole beforehand, the sensors too would have been visually blocked as were my eyes by the various obstacles at the street corner, such as the light post, fire hydrant, and so on. The radar of the self-driving car would not likely have gotten a good bounce off the street area around the corner. The LIDAR would have likewise likely not been able to detect the pothole. Etc.

Once the AI started to maneuver the self-driving car around the corner, it would then have a chance at detecting the pothole. Suppose the AI was not trained to do so or otherwise was not particularly setup to cope with potholes? In that case, the odds are that the AI would drive straight into the pothole and not even realize what was happening. All of a sudden, the self-driving car would be bumping and shoved to the side, all of which might be a complete mystery to the AI. The AI might even lose control of the self-driving car per se, allowing the self-driving car to drift over into someone else's lane or up onto the curb.

The AI might via the IMU (Inertial Measurement Unit) be able to realize that something is afoot when the overall balance of the self-driving was askew, but if it had not already detected the pothole it would be an unknown as to why the self-driving car has suddenly gone somewhat astray.

Would the AI be able to quickly enough counter the physics of the lurch caused by the hitting of the pothole?

Would it be able to correct for the shove that the self-driving car got by rolling into and over the pothole?

Even if it was able to detect the pothole in-advance of hitting it, would the AI be able to appropriately identify the alternatives such as swerving over or trying to come to a halt and assess the risks associated with those alternatives, thus making a "reasoned" selection of what to do?

These are serious questions regarding the driving capability of the AI.

I suppose some AI developers would assert that the AI has to be ready for potholes all the time anyway, and there isn't a special case involved in dealing with these roadway evils. Though this is partially true, it also belies the idea that with a crumbling infrastructure the pothole is going to no longer be a rare event of an edge case nature and will instead be a probably and frequent encounter.

The AI might need to cope with having to drive down any given street and be dodging a large crack in the street there, and a pothole over here, and then another pothole a few feet to the left, and maybe debris chopped out of a pothole by a prior car that hit the hole.

I tend to refer to this as the AI dodgeball mode. The AI needs to be able to play a kind of dodgeball game of maneuvering in and around the various obstacles and roadway problems. I doubt that most AI developers have considered ensuring that the AI can handle this somewhat repeated and continual effort of lots of dodges to be strung together, doing so while keeping the self-driving car safely on the road and not hit any other cars or nearby pedestrians.

In essence, the usual assumption is that the self-driving car will encounter one anomaly, the AI will be able to deal with it distinctly, and then if another anomaly appears it will be completely later in time, considered a separate occurrence and fully independent of the first encounter. The reality is that a lot of the roads are likely to be a morass of deterioration on a given road, often due to the heavy traffic on that particular road.

Also, as a road starts to deteriorate, it often accelerates in deterioration as there is a kind of momentum that a rough road gets rougher faster and sooner than might a road that otherwise is more resilient and not prone to getting beat-up. The rule-of-thumb is that a worsening road will tend toward getting worse, perhaps exponentially so. Worseness begets more worseness. Meanwhile, a road that is in good shape will likely be at first "resistant" to getting torn-up, and only once a threshold has been reached will it become the proverbial snowball that grows to become an avalanche of snow over time.

One aspect that might help AI self-driving cars to contend with banged-up roads is the use of V2V (vehicle-to-vehicle) electronic communications.

When I drove around the corner and hit the pothole, it would have been handy if I could have immediately communicated with the car behind me. I might have told the driver in the car behind me to watch out for the pothole. I might have also indicated that I was going to come to a sudden halt to avoid smashing into the hole, and thus I wanted them to not rear-end my car when I came to an unexpected halt.

With the use of V2V, one AI self-driving car could indeed tell another AI self-driving car to do those kinds of things. Presumably, in an orderly fashion, one AI helps another AI. Each self-driving car that follows the next would be forewarned about the pothole. This would also allow those AI self-driving cars to act in concert with each other, often referred to as a swarm, allowing each to avoid the pothole by making timed and coordinated maneuvers.

The one rub to this V2V is going to be the human drivers that are in the mix of the cars on the roads. Suppose that when I took the corner that I was in a Level 5 self-driving car and it tried to use to V2V to warn the car behind me. It could be that the car behind me was also a Level 5 self-driving car and it had V2V and it electronically listened to my self-driving car and abided by the suggested driving aspects. Or, it could be that a human driver was in the car behind me. Would they even receive the V2V? If they did receive the V2V would they opt to abide by the suggestions made by my AI of my self-driving car?

There is also the likely advent of V2I (vehicle-to-infrastructure) electronic communication. Suppose that there is a computing device somewhere near to the corner that I was turning at (these devices are sometimes referred to as edge computing devices). The device might have already gotten an indication that there is a pothole there at the corner and that it is scheduled to be repaired in a month's time. Meanwhile, it beacons out a message that there is a pothole and be wary of it. An AI self-driving car outfitted with the V2I would receive the message and be alerted to deal with the matter.

Part of the reason that the roadway infrastructure might hasten to deteriorate could partially be due to the advent of AI self-driving cars.

You might be shocked to think that the AI self-driving car emergence could somehow worsen the roadway infrastructure, since the AI is supposed to be a polite driver that obeys the laws and tries to drive as cleanly and legally as possible (I've debunked those assumptions, by the way!).

The reason that the advent of AI self-driving cars will likely exasperate the crumbling infrastructure is due to the belief that we'll want to use the AI self-driving cars non-stop. It is anticipated that AI self-driving cars will be used extensively for ridesharing purposes. You are at work during the day and allow your AI self-driving car to be making money for you while you are at the office. Likewise, at night time, while your head is nestled on your pillow in bed, your AI self-driving is out there making money.

The odds are that we are going to see a beehive of activity of self-driving cars cruising around night and day, waiting to pick-up and drop-off passengers. This continual driving is going to put more miles onto our already destitute roadways. More miles on falling apart roads means those roads will continue to fall apart. We can predict it will make those roads a lot worse. The constant pounding of self-driving car after self-driving car is a punishment that a crumbling infrastructure will not be able to readily withstand.

I suppose one potential good news is that the AI self-driving cars will hopefully make use of Machine Learning (ML) and be able to therefore increasingly get better at detecting lousy roads and sufficient driving on lousy roads. I had mentioned earlier the V2V of AI self-driving cars sharing with each other. Another form of sharing will be via OTA (Over-The-Air) electronic communication.

OTA consists of the AI self-driving car providing to the cloud of the auto maker or tech firm the data that the AI self-driving car is collecting while driving on the roads. This would include the camera data, video data, radar data, and so on. At the cloud level, the auto maker or tech firm can do analyses and try to use ML and deep learning to improve how the AI self-driving cars operate. These improvements can be pushed back down into the AI self-driving car, providing updates or patches for when something amiss in the software needs to be upgraded or fixed.

Let's consider again my pothole example. An AI self-driving car might already have been forewarned about the pothole because a prior AI self-driving car in the same fleet had reported it to the cloud via OTA. The aspect about this pothole was then brought back down into the rest of the AI self-driving cars in the fleet via the OTA too. Furthermore, beyond just having a mapped indication of where the pothole is, the Machine Learning aspects would have tried to figure out ways to contend with the pothole.

Thus, the AI self-driving cars in the fleet would not only be aware of the existence of the pothole, but also have some driving tactics and strategies to contend it with. Perhaps one aspect would be to not even make that right turn and go up another street to make the desired right turn. Another tactic might be to swing wide when making the turn, doing so by first warning the car next to the AI self-driving car. Each of these tactics would be contextually based, meaning that the choice is not always the same one, and instead that the context such as the time of day or the weather conditions might dictate which choice is the best at the moment of making the driving decision.

I've focused so far on having the AI be adept at contending with a crumbling infrastructure.

Perhaps I should not be so fatalistic. Let's imagine that we collectively have the willpower to do something substantive about the crumbling infrastructure.

Depending upon the status of AI self-driving cars at the juncture of moving forward on improving the infrastructure, we could use the data from the AI self-driving cars to better understand where the crumbling infrastructure is most occurring. Keep in mind that the AI self-driving cars will have their myriad of sensors and will be crisscrossing the roads and continually capturing visual images, radar, LIDAR, etc.

This is a huge amount of data that can be used to mine when trying to prioritize where to put our energies and monies on infrastructure improvements. This data can reveal which roads are most traveled and which are least traveled. It can reveal the roughness of the roads. There are a slew of handy analyses and metrics that can be discerned from this vast collection of data.

Another factor involves whether or not to merely fix the infrastructure as though we will continue to have only conventional cars, or whether to consider doing other kinds of improvements or upgrades to the infrastructure that tie into the advent of AI self-driving cars.

For example, I had mentioned herein the use of edge computing, which will be a boon to AI self-driving cars. Perhaps the crumbling infrastructure can be enhanced by the adoption of edge computing.

There is also going to be the OTA taking place and we need fast networks to handle that kind of data movement. I've already previously described the importance of 5G in my speeches and writings. Perhaps the infrastructure can include the adoption of 5G on a widespread basis across our roadways.

We will need a provision for dealing with AI self-driving cars that breakdown. I realize that some pundits claim that AI self-driving cars will never breakdown, but this is crazy talk. A car is a car. There will be lots of reasons for an AI self-driving car to breakdown, including as previously pointed out that they will be trying to run non-stop 24x7. We'll need to contend with the towing of broken-down AI self-driving cars, another topic that I've covered in my presentations and writings, and for which the infrastructure can be shaped to aid toward appropriately handling these situations.

Conclusion

With the existing roadway infrastructure that is falling apart at the seams, we need to be ready for the advent of AI self-driving cars. It would be a shame to have AI self-driving cars that cannot readily use what might be unpassable roads by the time that the AI is ready to hit the roads. Think of the irony that we might have in-hand self-driving cars, but they cannot go anyplace because of the marred roads. Or, we might put AI self-driving cars onto the roads, and their working for us non-stop causes the roads to hasten in crumbling.

One aspect involves making sure that the AI is savvy enough to be able to deal with the lousy infrastructure. There is though only so much that the AI can do in this regard. It would be like having all human drivers have to learn to gingerly drive so as to not unduly upset the roads. Better still would be to fix the infrastructure.

Fixing it means not just making what already exists passable, it also means that we would want to perform upgrades and improvements that dovetail with the emergence of AI self-driving cars. The motto often heard of "fix the darned roads" should be augmented by the clamor to "tech-up the roads" so that we'll have a synergistic effect of good tech-savvy roads that coincide with the prevalence of AI self-driving cars.

Come to think of it, I'm going to have some signs made-up that say this and stand at the pothole tomorrow to alert my fellow mankind of what we need to do next. Wave at me and honk your horn in support, would you please?

CHAPTER 3
E-BILLBOARDING
AND
AI SELF-DRIVING CARS

CHAPTER 3

E-BILLBOARDING
AND
AI SELF-DRIVING CARS

On my daily commute here in Southern California, I likely see about 20 to 30 billboards each way, each day. You might find of idle interest that there are an estimated 350,000 billboards throughout the United States. That's a lot of billboards!

Estimates of the amount of money spent on billboards annually in the U.S. vary, but many would guess it is around $8 billion dollars. In essence, those billboards that you drive past at 65 miles per hour, and for which maybe you notice and maybe you don't, they are big business involving big bucks. Advertisers seem to think that billboards are worth paying for. The companies that own billboards and seek out advertisers are of the belief that advertisers are wise to use billboards.

There are some billboards that are rather mundane and do not especially standout. I dare say that a number of the billboards are about trying to sell new cars and they often don't leap off the page, so to speak, and I wonder how much good those billboards are doing. Admittedly, these are billboards that are right next to the new car dealerships selling such cars, and so it is handy to have the billboard as a kind of "I'm here" signpost for anyone considering stopping to look at buying a new car.

One billboard that gets attention is one involving a mannequin of a cow on it, offering a 3D visualization that can catch the eye as you drive past it (you probably know the billboard, it is for a fast food chain that sells mainly chicken).

Another one that can be noticeable is an electronic one that is constantly changing from one image to another, and changes throughout the week. It is easy for the billboard company to showcase new items and avoid the usual labor-intensive act of having to put up a large-scale poster or otherwise do something physical when putting on a fresh ad for the billboard. These so-called electronic billboards, often referred to as e-billboards, offer the advantage of being easy and quick for displaying any new or changing ads.

If you've ever been to Times Square in New York City (NYC), you've undoubtedly seen the plethora of e-billboards displayed there. Some are amazed and watch the e-billboards in rapt attention. Others take a short look, shrug their shoulders, perceive it as a big glossy glowing mess, and don't look at it again. There are even protestors that say these kinds of electronic signs are a form of visual pollution. It is a blight on what we see around us. They go to Times Square and are sickened by what they see and assert that it should be banned or otherwise outlawed.

One of the billboards that is partially electronic that I notice each day during my commute is one that electronically displays the latest dollar number for the lottery. I admit it does get my attention. When the dollar amount is "low" such as a mere $50 million, I glance but take no particular action due to the billboard. When it gets to over $500 million, I become sheep like everyone else and opt to stop at a gas station to get a lottery ticket. I know it doesn't make much logical sense, given the crazy odds of winning, and that I should not become swept into the lottery ticket buying melees, but anyway I do, sorry to say.

Some people are happy that we are gradually shifting to electronic billboards since it dispenses with the use of paper, or canvas, or paints, and they would say that the e-billboards are better for the environment accordingly. Those that dislike billboards for the visual pollution tend to say that the electronic billboards are much worse in visual clutter than the traditional kinds of billboards.

Near the Los Angeles International Airport, known as LAX, there are several large buildings near the freeway that have huge canvas-like stretched material that nearly encompasses the whole building. These are essentially also billboards. Though the buildings were not built for the specific purpose of being a billboard, nonetheless they have been coopted into becoming billboards. The people inside the building can still readily see out their windows and thus this appears to be a handy way for the building owners to pick-up some extra dough.

When I do consulting work for the entertainment industry here in Hollywood and Burbank, I drive to the various studios each day. The major movie studios purposely rent billboards near to their studio lots (or buy up nearby billboards, or on their own they put up billboards near to their studios), and outfit the billboards with ads for their own movies and often post their movie stars pictures.

This makes sense in that if you were visiting that studio, you would encounter all of these fantastic ads about their movies, prior to arriving at the studio lot. The idea too is that if a move star is coming to the lot and the studio is pitching them to star in their movies, the more the movie star sees the billboards the presumption is that the movie star will get very excited about the pitch even before they arrive at the studio lot.

Imagine the other side of that coin. If you are a movie star headed to a studio owned by entertainment company X, and their competitor of entertainment company Y has rented up all the billboard space near to the studio lot of company X, you might have second thoughts about whether to do your movie with company X. You might think, well, perhaps I ought to be driving over to company Y instead. I don't know that the movie stars and movie makers really think that way, but the studios sure think they do.

I was recently in Las Vegas for the annual Consumer Electronics Show (CES), and throughout the Vegas famous Strip, which is a street that runs along the major casinos, there were numerous billboards. In addition to stationary billboards, such as those on a standalone basis and ones that were wrapped around buildings, there were also moving billboards. By moving billboards, I mean they were in motion. The billboard itself was moving – typically involving a truck that was towing the billboard and the billboard was mounted on wheels.

Some of the moving billboards were related to the CES conference and urging those attending to do something such as visit a particular casino or go see a particular show. Others of the moving billboards were apparently used on a regular basis for attracting attention to anyone that happens to be in Vegas. There were ads displayed for all kinds of aspects, including some that are unmentionable, while others were rather topical such as one for a financial service that could help you out of a financial jam (I suppose many of those gambling in Vegas might have found that billboard appealing).

These towed billboards can be a pain in the neck. I had my car there in Vegas and it was difficult to at times navigate near or around the trucks towing the billboards. Those moving billboards are large and bulky, and they tend to block the view of traffic. Such towed billboards can also "hide" pedestrians that are trying to jaywalk across a busy street. There are some that believe the towed billboards should be outlawed or banned.

A major reason to object to the moving billboards is that they can disrupt traffic flow. They can block views and create hazardous traffic related situations. You could also say that they are using up precious fuel and generating automotive pollutants for a somewhat questionable basis. It is one thing if you put a billboard on the side of a bus, since the bus is a form or public transportation and by using it for a billboard you are doing double duty. Having a truck that cruises around and around, doing nothing other than towing a billboard, it is something that many believe is improper and inappropriate.

This does bring up another facet that concerns many people about billboards altogether. They are a distraction. If you are driving on the freeway and see a billboard up ahead, which are going to do, focus on the roadway or instead look at the billboard? Indeed, the companies that advertise and the companies that own the billboard are hopeful that you will look at the billboard. They will do just about anything to get your eyeballs.

We therefore have a bit of a conundrum. Drivers are supposed to be focused on driving. Meanwhile, we allow these billboards to be setup near where we drive, which makes sense because where else will the eyeballs be found, and we let the billboard companies and advertisers try to have us shift our attention to their messaging.

Is it worth the potential of drivers taking their eyes off-the-road, and therefore presumably being less safe as drivers and increasing risks on our roadways, merely to be able to see a billboard that has perhaps a cow mannequin on it or a lottery dollar amount being displayed?

You could claim that drivers aren't looking at the billboards and that the billboards are really for the passengers in the cars. Yeh, right. That's a good one. You could claim that the drivers are already looking around anyway and that the distraction factor of seeing a billboard out of the corner of your eye is hardly any kind of distraction. You might like to read-up about some of the research studies that tend to suggest there is more risk involved than many might think.

If you want to claim that the billboards actually help drivers by having them become more visually engaged in their surroundings, I'd say that's going a bit far in trying to justify billboards. How many times have you heard about someone that happened to look at a billboard, which made them shift their gaze away from say their own navel, and so they were sparked into looking at the roadway and thank goodness the billboard was there. I've not heard much of that.

I've primarily so far been discussing what many refer to as Outdoor Advertising (OA), or sometimes referred to as Out-of-Home (OOH) advertising. There is advertising that you might see while inside an airport such as LAX, plastered on the walls and with standalone kiosks throughout the terminal areas. I'm herein mainly focusing on the kind of billboards and ads that you see while outdoors such as nearby to highways, freeways, and streets.

There are the large outdoor advertising stands that are a physical structure and have a movie-screen sized poster or similar pictorial display. I've also mentioned that some now are electronic displays. I'm going to call them e-billboards, though some refer to them as Digital Billboards (DBB) or possibly Digital Out-of-the-Home (DOOH) displays.

One question to ponder is this – do they work?

The billboard industry continually tries to hammer away at the claim that these outdoor billboards do work. What does that mean? They would claim that people notice the billboards and that it ultimately leads to buying behaviors. I see a billboard for a new movie, and I opt that next weekend to go see the movie at the movie theatre. I see a billboard for a new hair jell, and I go to the store the next day and get buy some. In essence, the claim is that there is a correlation between your seeing the billboard and your likelihood of then making a purchase decision because of it.

Not all billboards necessarily lead to an immediate reward for the advertising firm. Maybe the billboard is intended simply for brand awareness. You might not be buying that brand anytime in the near future. Hopefully though, when you are ready to make a purchase related to the item, you have planted in your mind that particular firm or product and it will urge you to purchase their product.

I've had some people that come visit me here in SoCal that look intently at the billboards and tell me that half of the billboards mention items that they would never purchase. As such, they tell me that those billboards are a waste. I gently point out that the billboards are not intended to get every person on earth to be prompted by the billboard. In other words, a billboard might be displaying an ad that only a segment of those seeing the billboard will believe it pertains to them.

There are billboards here that tout some of our local gambling casinos and point out that you don't need to drive five or six hours to Vegas to go gambling. I know people that refuse to gamble. For them, the billboard is perhaps a waste. But, others that see the billboard and are interested in gambling might say to themselves, hey, I didn't realize I could gamble within 30 minutes of where I now am, I'll go there soon.

You could even make the case that those that don't gamble might pass along the ad to others that they know. Perhaps you aren't a gambler yourself, but your relatives love to gamble, and they are coming to Los Angeles next week. Based on seeing the billboard, you might tell them that they can go gambling at the local casino. Though you originally perceived that the billboard was wasted on you, it turns out that you got the message and relayed it to others. I'd say that suggests the billboard wasn't truly wasted on you. It had a payoff.

Another way to answer the question as to whether they work or not might be the simplest explanation, namely that they exist therefore they must work. Is that some kind of tortured tautology? Well, not exactly. The point being that if advertisers did not believe the billboards worked, they presumably would not be willing to spend money on them. There are lots of other ways to spend advertising dollars, such as on radio ads, TV ads, online ads, and so on.

Admittedly, some companies run the ads on billboards due to the aspect that they want to say they have billboard ads. You are doing it kind of for bragging rights. This notion that you are running billboard ads might be an element of your portraying your firm as a significant company. Whether people actually go ahead and buy your product because of the billboards, you might not especially care. It would be nice if it had that kind of impact, but if it only is serving as a promotional tool in other ways, you might be fine with that aspect too.

I knew one driver that said he refused to look at billboards. He didn't like them. He didn't like them in a box, he didn't like them with a fox (thanks goes to Dr. Seuss!). He said they were ugly and a blight on society. He felt that if he looked at a billboard, any billboard, it would make the advertiser encouraged to make use of even more billboards. By averting his eyes, he was doing his part to discourage billboards and hoped that it would someday lead to the death knell of billboards. He was a hard case on this topic, for sure.

I don't want to burst his bubble, but I think we all know his attempts to avert his eyes did not move the needle in terms of disrupting the billboard industry. If he had tried to go the route of saying that the billboards were distracting and a hazard to driving, he might have been able to make the case for his averting of his eyes. I'd say that people would be more willing to buy into his protests in that case.

What's your opinion about billboards? Love them? Hate them? Tolerate them? Like them in moderation? Find them essential, funny, heartwarming, touching, informative, and can't wait to see them? Or, believe they should be put into a junk heap and burned? There are all kinds of views on the matter.

What does this have to do with AI self-driving cars?

At the Cybernetic AI Self-Driving Car Institute, we are developing AI software for self-driving cars. One arising aspect involves the potential for e-billboarding becoming a significant element of AI self-driving cars.

Allow me to elaborate.

I'd like to first clarify and introduce the notion that there are varying levels of AI self-driving cars. The topmost level is considered Level 5. A Level 5 self-driving car is one that is being driven by the AI and there is no human driver involved. For the design of Level 5 self-driving cars, the auto makers are even removing the gas pedal, brake pedal, and steering wheel, since those are contraptions used by human drivers. The Level 5 self-driving car is not being driven by a human and nor is there an expectation that a human driver will be present in the self-driving car. It's all on the shoulders of the AI to drive the car.

For self-driving cars less than a Level 5, there must be a human driver present in the car. The human driver is currently considered the responsible party for the acts of the car. The AI and the human driver are co-sharing the driving task. In spite of this co-sharing, the human is supposed to remain fully immersed into the driving task and be ready at all times to perform the driving task. I've repeatedly warned about the dangers of this co-sharing arrangement and predicted it will produce many untoward results.

Let's focus herein on the true Level 5 self-driving car. Much of the comments apply to the less than Level 5 self-driving cars too, but the fully autonomous AI self-driving car will receive the most attention in this discussion.

Here's the usual steps involved in the AI driving task:

- Sensor data collection and interpretation
- Sensor fusion
- Virtual world model updating
- AI action planning
- Car controls command issuance

Another key aspect of AI self-driving cars is that they will be driving on our roadways in the midst of human driven cars too. There are some pundits of AI self-driving cars that continually refer to a utopian world in which there are only AI self-driving cars on the public roads. Currently there are about 250+ million conventional cars in the United States alone, and those cars are not going to magically disappear or become true Level 5 AI self-driving cars overnight.

Indeed, the use of human driven cars will last for many years, likely many decades, and the advent of AI self-driving cars will occur while there are still human driven cars on the roads. This is a crucial point since this means that the AI of self-driving cars needs to be able to contend with not just other AI self-driving cars, but also contend with human driven cars. It is easy to envision a simplistic and rather unrealistic world in which all AI self-driving cars are politely interacting with each other and being civil about roadway interactions. That's not what is going to be happening for the foreseeable future. AI self-driving cars and human driven cars will need to be able to cope with each other.

Returning to the topic of e-billboards, let's consider how this matter relates to the advent of AI self-driving cars.

First, be aware that there are pundits on both sides of the issue about what will ultimately happen to billboards once we have prevalent AI self-driving cars. There are the pessimists that say billboards will gradually disappear and you won't see them alongside our roadways anymore, while there are the optimists that claim the billboard will flourish though in ways different from the billboards of today.

Let's consider these two divergent viewpoints.

Why might billboards become a lost art and die off? Here's why. If we are all ensconced in our AI self-driving cars, it is believed that we will sleep in them, we will work while inside them, and that otherwise we will be visually entertained and our focus will be nearly exclusively on the interior of the self-driving car.

There is no particular reason to look out the car windows when you are in a true Level 5 self-driving car because the AI is doing the driving and you don't need to pay attention to the roadway (that's the theory of it). In fact, you probably don't really want windows at all and instead would use that same area to have LED displays. This would allow you to have your favorite online video streaming on one of the "windows" (now a display), while maybe doing a Skype-like session via the use of the space on another "window" and so on.

You might be thinking that with no windows you might get claustrophobic. Well, via the LED displays, you could simply have the AI display whatever the car camera sensors are seeing. You don't need to roll down an actual window.

You can instead "look outside" by tapping into the cameras on the self-driving car. But the odds are that you will rarely be looking "outside" and will be preoccupied with using the displays for other purposes, either for work, for studying, for doing live meetings with others, etc.

Some companies are going to be making car windows that can be readily electronically made to switch from being transparent to being opaque. This would allow you to use those car windows for either acting as internal LED displays or to be used to look outside of the car. Others though say that these switchable kinds of windows will come and go (falling out of favor), and eventually there won't be any windows at all. The use of window will be considered as a lesser safe aspect of the self-driving car, a weakness, which can get smashed and toss glass everywhere. There are those that say we'll be better off without the windows and instead use that space with a more hardened material.

If this prediction is correct, it means that the billboards that are alongside our roadways won't be seen by anyone that's inside a car. As mentioned earlier, today's billboards survive and succeed when they attract eyeballs. No eyeballs, no point in paying to put your advertisement on the billboard. No paying advertisers means the billboard companies won't make money. Billboard companies not making money will let their old-time billboards languish, and they'll become relics.

Here's another nail in the coffin for those outdoor billboards. If you are focusing your attention inside of the self-driving car, advertisers are going to fight to get onto the LED displays inside the self-driving car.

When taking a cab these days, if you've perchance accidentally or by old-habits done so versus using a ridesharing service, you'll notice that most "modern day" cabs have displays that show advertisements. These used to be small-sized posters that were taped to the back of the front seats of the cab, and now they are tablet sized LED displays.

The ridesharing services have been somewhat reluctant to go the same path as the cab companies in terms of showcasing ads via inside-the-car displays. Executives at the ridesharing firms don't want to irk their ridesharing customers. Though the ads would be a tempting amount of revenue, if it curtailed the growth rate of the ridesharing firms it would not be worth the incremental revenue. Most of the ridesharing services are losing money anyway, and they just need to keep touting their number of passengers and their adoption growth rate (whether they make money is apparently not important to anyone as yet, it's instead all about market share!).

In a quick recap of the pessimist's viewpoint, you won't be looking outside of your AI self-driving car, and therefore there's no eyeballs or very few eyeballs on those outdoor billboards. Furthermore, as a double whammy, the advertisers are going to divert their spending to getting "inside" the AI self-driving car and being displayed on your internal displays. In that sense, the advertisers will abandon the outdoor billboards. It's a one-two knockout punch to the outdoor billboards industry.

Does all of this mean that you should be dumping your stock in billboard companies? Well, let's hear what the other side of the coin has to say. We need to give the optimists a chance to speak their piece.

The optimists say that the glory days of billboards are yet upon us. The slight twist will be that the billboards will become predominantly e-billboards. These e-billboards will do much more than the ones of today.

Suppose you are in your AI self-driving car and heading to work. Your AI self-driving car is likely using V2V (vehicle-to-vehicle) electronic communications to communicate with other nearby self-driving cars. This will allow the various self-driving cars around your self-driving car to coordinate their activities. If one of the self-driving cars detects debris up ahead in the rightmost lane, it can quickly inform the other AI systems of the upcoming self-driving cars. Those AI systems would then presumably try to get out of the rightmost lane so as to avoid hitting the debris.

These V2V transmissions can be picked-up by essentially anyone or anything that is nearby. The billboard company might have edge computing devices that are attached to their outdoor billboard or that are nearby the billboard. These edge computing devices are keeping tabs on the V2V communications.

This might allow the e-billboard that you are about to drive past to suddenly be changed to display an image or video that applies to you, or maybe to those around you in nearby self-driving cars. The Machine Learning (ML) or Deep Learning (DL) system being used by the billboard company is collecting tons of data while self-driving cars are streaming along on the freeway, and the ML and DL is able to try and figure out which ads are best to be placed on the e-billboard display. This can change too from moment to moment, all depending upon the pattern of the traffic and who is driving past the e-billboard.

What about the idea that you'll be in your self-driving car as an enclosed shell and won't be looking outside? Nonsense say the optimists. You are not going to coop yourself up in your self-driving car. You are going to want to look outside. Whereas before, while you were driving a car, you could not enjoy the luxury of looking around. Now that all human drivers are no longer drivers, and they are relegated instead to being passengers, they will lovingly welcome being able to look outside of their self-driving car.

Indeed, these proponents would say that people are not going to feel comfortable with not looking outside and otherwise blindly trusting the AI to drive the car. Furthermore, these occupants might want to change the course of the driving journey and opt to have the AI self-driving car stop at that Starbucks up ahead, which they just realized was there by having noticed the e-billboard that mentioned it.

There might also be an electronic connection going on between the e-billboards and your in-car LED displays. As you get within eyesight of the e-billboard, it pops up a small message on your interior LED display that says you've got to take a look at the magnificent e-billboard image that you are about to drive past. You look at the e-billboard. Amazing, you think. You wonder how you could learn more about the product being showcased. At that moment, you look back at your internal LED display and see a convenient link shown there, allowing you to click on it and be provided with a lot more detail about the product.

Another factor is the predicted non-stop use of AI self-driving cars. Presumably, AI self-driving cars will be going all day and all night long. Ridesharing services will provide them. You can even buy your own AI self-driving car and have it listed as a ridesharing service, allowing you to make money via your AI self-driving car. Thus, while at work, your self-driving car is doing ridesharing and making money. After your AI self-driving car drops you at home upon the end of your workday, it goes out for the night and the wee morning hours, making you more money.

Why care about this aspect? It could imply that there are going to be even more eyeballs for billboard watching. People that don't use a car today or rarely use one will potentially readily use AI self-driving cars as a ridesharing medium. So you've now turned the human drivers into passengers with eyeballs to watch billboards, and you are adding more people to traveling in cars (self-driving cars), which puts more eyeballs within range of seeing the billboards (mainly e-billboards).

It is a kind of eyeball growth nirvana. Billboard companies will likely add more billboards, and fight to put more of them up alongside roadways. That's what the optimists say will happen.

As an aside, remember how I earlier suggested that advertisers don't necessarily know whether people are really looking at their billboards? The billboard companies do various kinds of surveys to try and find out from people whether they have looked at a billboard, but this is a rather crude and at times questionable way to really accurately indicate whether people are looking at the billboards or not.

Here's a twist for you. AI self-driving cars are going to be outfitted with cameras that point inward, allowing whomever is inside the AI self-driving car to be captured on video. Ridesharing firms will do this to protect the self-driving cars and be able to know if someone is messing around by destroying the interior or writing graffiti on the interior car walls.

The twist is that the billboard company could ask the auto maker or tech firm to report whether people gazed at the billboard as the self-driving car went past it. This would be easy data to collect.

The OTA (Over-the-Air) electronic connection between the self-driving car and the auto maker or tech firm cloud will be uploading data from the self-driving car, doing so to aid the auto maker or tech firm in analyzing the data and presumably improving the AI systems of the self-driving car (the OTA can allow them to push updates and patches to the AI of the self-driving car).

All the auto maker or tech firm needs to do is setup an automated system that would scan through the uploaded video of the interior facing camera and do a search for the time whenever the self-driving car went past the billboard. At that point in the video, the automated system could readily detect the faces of the people inside the AI self-driving car. This detection could also examine whether the faces are looking outside the self-driving car and whether their eyes and gaze seemed to be in the direction of the e-billboard.

Now that's quantitative data!

Which camp are you in?

Do you think that the pessimists are correct, and the billboard industry is doomed? Or, do you believe the optimists are on the right track and the billboard industry is heading to a grand resurgence? Both arguments seem rather compelling.

I'd add some additional aspects that might either help clear things up or maybe just make the waters even murkier.

I've already mentioned that the interior of the self-driving car might end-up having its own variant of e-billboards. Though ridesharing services aren't doing so particular now, it is a safe bet that in the future they will be.

I'd wager that if you bought an AI self-driving car and you opted to have it be a ridesharing service when you weren't otherwise using it, you'd welcome the added revenue that you could get by allowing for ads to be pumped into your AI self-driving car interior LED displays.

There are some that are even suggesting that the ridesharing services will get really inexpensive or maybe even become free-of-charge to the passengers, doing so to get eyeballs into the self-driving cars that will then see the interior displayed adds. If you are an advertiser, isn't it great to know that someone will be trapped inside a AI self-driving car for their driving journey and have no choice but to see your video that proudly advertisers your product? Gotta love those captive audiences.

I'll now provide the added element that I've not yet mentioned but could be a bonanza. What about the exterior of the AI self-driving car?

Suppose we place on the exterior of the AI self-driving car an electronic billboard or maybe a series of them all around the outside of the vehicle. The AI self-driving car now becomes a moving billboard, akin to what I had mentioned earlier that I had seen in Vegas. The good news is that the e-billboard of the AI self-driving car is presumably doing double-duty in that the AI self-driving car is also carrying occupants, similar to how the buses with billboards are doing double-duty.

In other words, if the AI self-driving car is taking someone from point A to point B, why not also be displaying electronic ads on the outside of the self-driving car too. This would be relatively easy to arrange. The OTA of the self-driving car could get ads pumped down to the AI self-driving car. These ads could change depending upon where the AI self-driving car is headed.

For example, suppose you are taking the AI self-driving car to the baseball stadium, so you can watch a baseball game that will be played there.

The AI realizes that you are heading to the baseball stadium. There are going to be lots of other cars nearby with people also heading to the baseball game. There will be baseball avid pedestrians too, once your AI self-driving car gets closer to the stadium.

Seems like an advertiser that wants to catch the eyeballs of baseball-going people will relish having their video ads placed onto your exterior displays. Rather than having just any kind of ads, this would allow the advertiser to target their ads to the specifics of baseball goers. Maybe a company that makes baseball gloves and bats would want to run an ad. Perhaps a gym service would run an ad, figuring that the people seeing the ad are more likely to be athletic and might go to a gym to workout.

Here's another neat trick. The sensors of the AI self-driving car are detecting the presence of pedestrians and other cars, doing so to properly drive the self-driving car. You could readily use that same data to spot whether people are looking at the displays on the outside of the AI self-driving car. Once again, we have a means to easily provide a quantitative measure of whether the ads are actually being seen by people.

Seems like a win-win.

You might wonder why today's cars aren't being outfitted with e-billboard like displays. One reason could be that the displays would be criticized as being distracting to human drivers. In a future of all AI self-driving cars, there aren't any human drivers that would be distracted. You could have the displays and ads go nuts and showcase whatever splashy content they wanted (within the bounds of whatever legal limits there might be).

Of course, if the passengers in self-driving cars are not going to be looking outside, this cuts out a lot of the eyeballs that might be watching those exterior self-driving car displays. You would still have the pedestrians presumably to look at the displays. Whether that's sufficient or not is an open question.

We are back to the money-making side of things too.

If you've bought an expensive AI self-driving car and you are desperate to make money to afford it, I'd bet that you'd be fine with displaying ads on the exterior of the AI self-driving car. Indeed, you might be more comfortable displaying ads on the outside versus the insider. The problem with displaying the ads on the inside is that you might have riders that don't like seeing ads and will avoid using your ridesharing service. There might be ridesharing services that tout the fact that they do not display ads inside their AI self-driving cars, which they hope will then attract riders over other AI self-driving cars that do allow ads (almost like differentiating between allowing smoking versus a non-smoking car).

Some wonder whether these external displays might confuse the sensors of the AI self-driving cars.

Here's what they mean. Suppose your AI self-driving car is heading along on the freeway and there is another self-driving car ahead of it. This other self-driving car has a big display at the rear of the car and can be seen readily by anyone behind the AI self-driving car.

The display suddenly shows a mad bull that seems to rushing toward you. It's only a video. But, perhaps the camera on your AI self-driving car does not realize this is merely a video and does an image analysis and concludes that a mad bull is charging directly at the AI self-driving car. This gets conveyed to the AI Action Planning portion of the system, and all of sudden the AI is commanding your self-driving car to make a radical and risky lane change to get away from the charging bull. Oops, shame on the AI.

I know you might laugh at this notion. Perhaps the charging bull is not the most serious way to express the dangers. The point though is that it is presumably a possibility that the displays on various nearby AI self-driving cars might visually overwhelm or confuse or confound the sensors of the other nearby AI self-driving cars. As such, one could lob the same kind of criticism about distracting human drivers, which instead that these displays could "distract" (maybe confuse or fool) the AI system of the self-driving car.

That being said, many pundits of AI self-driving cars would say that any self-respecting AI self-driving car that might get confused by an electronic display that is nearby shouldn't be on the roadway to begin with. If it is that easy to confuse or fool the AI, the AI doesn't deserve to be driving a self-driving car. For them, this suggestion that ad e-billboards on self-driving cars might be a danger to driving is a non-starter and they reject the notion entirely.

There are some that envision that the AI of a self-driving car make have a different kind of vantage about dealing with the e-billboard displays. Suppose you let your AI self-driving car know that you are a beer drinker. You love drinking beer. While you are in your AI self-driving car, the AI is using its sensors to detect other cars and pedestrians.

Imagine if the AI is also examining the e-billboards and scanning them to see what kinds of ads are being displayed. On the self-driving car up ahead, it is displaying a beer ad. The AI notifies you to look up and glance at the self-driving car in the lane to the right. You do so. You see a beer ad. Nice, it was just the kind of ad you'd like to see.

Some people are coming up with other imaginative ideas. You might have your own virtual avatar, and you display it on your exterior displays. Anyone watching your self-driving car will know that "superman" or "superwoman" (your chosen avatar) is in that self-driving car. Or, maybe you sell your own fresh-squeezed juices and you use your exterior displays to advertise your own product. And so on.

Conclusion

For billboard companies, it could be the best of times or it could be the worst of times, and the advent of AI self-driving cars might be the determiner of which way things will go. Will we end-up with roadside e-billboards or will they not make the cut. Will we end-up with e-billboards on the exterior of our AI self-driving cars?

For those of you that already don't like the visual clutter or visual pollution of billboards, pretend for a moment that all 250+ million cars in the United States are eventually replaced by AI self-driving cars and that they all have exterior e-billboards displays. This means that wherever those self-driving cars go, you can have the same kind of visual cacophony of Times Square, all the time, anywhere.

If this makes you shudder, I guess you'll want to never look outside of your AI self-driving car. Plus, when walking around as a pedestrian, perhaps wear some kind of special Augmented Reality (AR) glasses that are able to block out the e-billboards that are flashing and glaring all around you. Until this is all figured out, I'm voting that nobody runs an ad with a charging bull as part of their exterior displays on any AI self-driving cars. Ole!

CHAPTER 4

KINSHIP
AND
AI SELF-DRIVING CARS

CHAPTER 4

KINSHIP

AND AI SELF-DRIVING CARS

The famous Heidelberg manuscript from the 13th century indicates that kin-blood is not spoiled by water. In more modern times, we've come to express this as the now-classic saying that blood is thicker than water. Whichever way you might prefer to state it, the underlying notion is that bloodline family and familial relationships are considered a very strong bond. Indeed, some would assert that the familial bonds are stronger than any other kind of friendship or relationship that you might ever formulate. Family and bloodline trumps over anything else, in their view.

If you look at history there is certainly a lot of credence to this postulation about kinship. Humans have often had to make tough choices in life and at times seemed to choose the bloodline even when it might have been more sensible to not do so. Animals seem to also have a familial tendency and you can readily watch online videos of wild animals that will take great chances to save or protect their own bloodline offspring.

Many movies and stories abound about how someone got into hot water by giving a job to a bloodline relative that otherwise likely wasn't qualified for the role. Today's news covers instances of wealthy founders that control large-scale conglomerates and how they put their family connections over the top of any other business dealings. There seems to be a magnetic power that attracts and bonds by kinship.

It is difficult to clearly say why this kinship aspect matters so much. Why should the fact that someone else has the same bloodline as you make such a difference? One would assume that how people treat each other, and the other facets of human-to-human relationships, would determine the bonding type and level of formulation. Acts and deeds would presumably be the highest sign of creating a bond. But, somehow, we nonetheless still often resort back to the seemingly simplistic matter of bloodline.

Those that study the nature of evolution and abide by Darwin's theories would suggest that it is rather apparent why the bloodline would be so revered. When you are faced with the basics of survival, you need to have others that can protect your back. By becoming a kind of pack, your chances of survival are presumably enhanced. The question then becomes whom can you or should you form a pack with? In a rudimentary caveman or cavewoman manner, it would have made sense to focus on your own bloodline.

One aspect is that your own bloodline would be a known more so than an unknown. Those with your bloodline were more likely to have similar characteristics as you. They would tend toward the same physical attributes and presumably similar cognitive and personality attributes. This would appear to make the connectivity of the pack a more likely magnetic or attracting element and promote cohesiveness. Strangers would be less likely to stick out their neck to help you, while your own type would perhaps be more willing to go the extra mile for your sake.

I'd wager that we all can see the logic of this bloodline calculation. Does it still make sense today, in a modern world? One might argue that it is a legacy carryover from the days of basic survival. It might not provide any much value or protection in a modern age. Or, perhaps it still does and in spite of your modern conveniences of life, the foundational familial bond still is essential. No matter how space age we become, it could be that the kinship rule will always still apply.

Here's a twist for you: What about plants?

Do plants have a similar kinship aspect? Would a plant be willing to aid more so its own bloodline of plants, doing so over a non-bloodline plant?

I think that most of us would say it is preposterous to suggest that plants would have a kinship. Plants aren't people. Plants aren't animals. Plants are, well, they are plants. They don't know what they are doing. They don't know how to act towards others. At a quick glance, it would seem that plants cannot possibly abide by any kind of bloodline familial kinship. The idea itself is presumably outlandish.

There is a growing contingent of plant evolutionary ecologists that would claim you are wrong in your assumption about plants.

Over ten years ago, a researcher at McMaster University published a paper that there are plants that seem to exhibit kinship behaviors. Since then, there has been a back-and-forth of fellow researchers trying to further prove the contention and others that have tried to debunk it.

What kinds of research findings provide support for the plant kinship theory?

It has been suggested that plants will spread their roots when around non-bloodline plants and will tend to rein in their roots when nearby to bloodline plants. This willingness to narrow the reach of the roots is an indicator that the plant is keen to allow other nearby plants a greater chance to survive and extend their own roots. If the plant extends its roots, it is saying that the war is on and other nearby plants will need to compete with the root system of the spreading plant. Apparently, one might conclude, the plant is narrowing its roots to support kinships, while not narrowing its roots when surrounded by non-kinship relationships.

That does seem interesting. Is it a compelling case? Those opposed to the assertion that kinship is involved would say that there are other ways to explain the phenomena. It could be that the roots of a like matter are simply prohibiting the roots of the other plant to reach out. Meanwhile, roots of a different kind do not have the same mechanism and so the plant is spreading out into their territory. The claim of a form of causation based on kinship is misleading, some would say, and it is merely a matter of whether the plants are of a like type or not.

Here's another plant example of potential kinship. Some studies show that a plant will shift the angle and direction of its leaves to reduce the impact of shadows being cast onto another nearby plant. This helps the nearby plant by ensuring that it gets more sunshine and nourishment therefore via the sun. And guess what? Yes, you probably guessed that supposedly plants of the same kinship were more likely to alter their leaves positioning, aiding other nearby plants of their own familial line. They tended to not do so for other non-kinship plants.

Further proof that plants form kinships? Maybe, maybe not.

These alleged kinship effects are being described as altruistic. An individual plant will appear to forego some of its own chances of survival to aid the chances of survival for its kin. One might say that the online videos of lions willing to attack hyenas that are attacking a kin are quite similar. It seems overly risky for a lion to enter into the fray and attempt to knock back the hyenas, doing so at great personal risk. They seem to do this as spurred by their kinship and bloodline effects.

A recent study of plants by researchers at the University of Lausanne indicated that after growing over 700 seedlings in pots, some of which were alone in a pot and others that had up to six nearby neighbors, the kinship plants in a pot apparently sprouted more flowers. This is a handy survival and thriving action because the more flowers there are then the more chances of alluring to the plants of pollinators. The more pollinators then the greater the chances of continuing the plant legacy.

To make those added flowers, each plant would need to consume a greater amount of energy and therefore be somewhat sacrificing itself for the greater collective good. The more crowded a pot was with kinship plants, the more the flowers were blooming.

Again, is this absolute proof of kinship in plants? You could argue that it does not provide irrefutable evidence for it. We might be back to the notion that some plants have inherent mechanisms that come to play when nearby other kinds of plants. Perhaps we could use other kinds of plants that aren't of a kinship nature, but for which they have similar attributes, and maybe get the same results.

Indeed, there is a viewpoint that sometimes kinships draws kin together, while it does not draw-in non-kinships, or might even go further and attempt to undermine or repel non-kinships. In other words, we might fight for our kin. We might not go out of our way to fight for our non-kin. We might also fight to keep at bay our non-kin. This means we are overtly rejecting non-kin, rather than simply trying to accept or aid our own kin.

Throughout all of this, you might be asking yourself how in the world does one plant even know whether another plant is a kin or not a kin?

With humans, we can talk with each other, we can look at each other, we can touch each other, and otherwise use our various senses to try and figure out a kin versus a non-kin. You might say that lions can do the same, though perhaps not do the talking part (though, they can make vocalizations that would allow for a like-kind use of sounds as a communication medium).

Among the plant kinship believers, one idea is that plants emit chemical indicators and those chemotypes can be a signal to other plants. This might be emitted on the leaves, stalk, and via the roots of the plant, allowing for communicating above and below ground. It could be a kin recognition signal. Another idea is that it could be via light, since plants tend to have light-related sensors. All told, there are more ways for plants to possibly communicate than you might have at first considered.

Not everyone is on-board the plant kinship train. Disputes about the research designs are ongoing. Those that are proponents of the kinship theories are apt to also offer new ideas about how to exploit the feature. Knowing that a kinship exists, you could apparently leverage the capability to more readily regrow or regenerate a forest that has been undermined. In any case, the plant kinship debate will likely continue for a while and we'll have to wait and see how it plays out.

What does this have to do with AI self-driving cars?

At the Cybernetic AI Self-Driving Car Institute, we are developing AI software for self-driving cars. One interesting aspect will be how various AI self-driving cars act toward each other, for which there might be a kinship element involved.

Allow me to elaborate.

I'd like to first clarify and introduce the notion that there are varying levels of AI self-driving cars. The topmost level is considered Level 5. A Level 5 self-driving car is one that is being driven by the AI and there is no human driver involved. For the design of Level 5 self-driving cars, the auto makers are even removing the gas pedal, brake pedal, and steering wheel, since those are contraptions used by human drivers. The Level 5 self-driving car is not being driven by a human and nor is there an expectation that a human driver will be present in the self-driving car. It's all on the shoulders of the AI to drive the car.

For self-driving cars less than a Level 5, there must be a human driver present in the car. The human driver is currently considered the responsible party for the acts of the car. The AI and the human driver are co-sharing the driving task. In spite of this co-sharing, the human is supposed to remain fully immersed into the driving task and be ready at all times to perform the driving task. I've repeatedly warned about the dangers of this co-sharing arrangement and predicted it will produce many untoward results.

Let's focus herein on the true Level 5 self-driving car. Much of the comments apply to the less than Level 5 self-driving cars too, but the fully autonomous AI self-driving car will receive the most attention in this discussion.

Here's the usual steps involved in the AI driving task:

- Sensor data collection and interpretation
- Sensor fusion
- Virtual world model updating
- AI action planning
- Car controls command issuance

Another key aspect of AI self-driving cars is that they will be driving on our roadways in the midst of human driven cars too. There are some pundits of AI self-driving cars that continually refer to a utopian world in which there are only AI self-driving cars on the public roads. Currently there are about 250+ million conventional cars in the United States alone, and those cars are not going to magically disappear or become true Level 5 AI self-driving cars overnight.

Indeed, the use of human driven cars will last for many years, likely many decades, and the advent of AI self-driving cars will occur while there are still human driven cars on the roads. This is a crucial point since this means that the AI of self-driving cars needs to be able to contend with not just other AI self-driving cars, but also contend with human driven cars. It is easy to envision a simplistic and rather unrealistic world in which all AI self-driving cars are politely interacting with each other and being civil about roadway interactions. That's not what is going to be happening for the foreseeable future. AI self-driving cars and human driven cars will need to be able to cope with each other.

Returning to the notion of kinship and familial relationships, let's consider how this kind of element might come to play regarding the advent of AI self-driving cars.

Suppose you are driving your car on a busy highway. Your daughter is driving her car and is just ahead of you in traffic. You catch-up with her and realize that she is going to try and make a right turn into an upcoming shopping center.

The highway traffic is moving at a fast clip and you realize that when she tries to make the right turn, it will necessitate her potentially having to make the right turn very quickly so as to not slowdown traffic. Making such a turn rapidly might not be a good idea and could lead to her potentially hitting a pedestrian or another car that is near to the entrance into the shopping center where she is going to make her turn. You are also worried that when she starts to make the right turn, a car from behind her on the highway might be impatient and fail to notice that she is going to make a turn and might ram into her car.

Therefore, you decide to stay directly behind her and when she approaches the point of the turn, you opt to especially slowdown, pump your brakes, and otherwise try to block the traffic in your lane. This is a means of trying to help her make the turn. It is almost like playing football, wherein one player blocks others to allow the quarterback to make their move. You are creating a kind of traffic buffer so that she can make the right turn at a more measured pace and to prevent other highway traffic from potentially pressuring her or possibly even hitting her car.

What a great parent you are!

I'd like to now change the scenario just a tad. Suppose the same situation arises, but this time the driver in the car ahead of you is unknown to you. As far as you know, the driver is a complete stranger. How might that alter your actions?

Well, it could be that you are already late getting to work and the traffic has been very frustrating for you. All sorts of idiots drivers seem to be the road today. Worse still, it is raining, and this has caused traffic to go slower than normal. You are fed up with the drivers! You are fed up with those that are getting in your way as you drive! Everyone should get off the road and let you proceed.

You are driving in the right lane and all of sudden you realize that the driver in the car directly ahead of you is going to try and make a right turn into the shopping center. This dolt doesn't seem to realize it is a tough turn to make and will likely cause traffic in the lane to have to slowdown. Not another dolt driving a car!

You move up to the bumper of the car and try to pressure them into having second thoughts about making the turn. Meanwhile, you are eyeballing the lane to your left and trying to decide if you can deftly swing into that lane and avoid having to slow down due to the inconsiderate driver that's going to be making the right turn. You realize that you might be able to sneak into the lane to the left, though it will likely cause the driver in the car behind you to be suddenly surprised at discovering the car ahead is going to make the turn into the shopping center.

Maybe the driver behind you might even smash into the dolt. Fine. That's two less cars on the roadway today. The driver making the turn might get a harsh lesson in how to properly drive on the highway and streets of your town. The driver behind you that perhaps smacks into the other car, well, that driver is likely a bad driver too. The two bad drivers deserve each other.

That second scenario is a doozy.

In the first scenario, you were willing to move the earth and the moon to support your daughter as she was wanting to make the turn into the shopping center. In the second scenario, you could care less about the stranger driving the car ahead of you and indeed you felt it was wrong on their part to even consider or attempt the turn.

We might say that your kinship shaped your driving behavior.

I know that it seems a bit contrived and you might object to how I setup the scenario. I'll grant you that aspect. My overarching point was that you might alter your driving behavior depending on whom is driving in another car, rather than on the driving task or situation per se.

In other words, if you know the person that is driving a car that is near you, you might well change how you drive, depending upon what your "relationship" might be associated with that person. I think we can all agree this seems plausible. I would even say it is more than plausible, it is probable that you would change your driving behavior.

I realize there are some sticklers out there that will claim they always drive the same way. They are always courteous and fair to other drivers. Always. Or, maybe they are always a jerk to other drivers and won't change their driving behavior for anyone. They don't care who is in the other cars. By gosh, they are going to drive as they drive, all the time, the way they do, and continue to cut-off other drivers and treat them like dirt.

I'd bet that most of us do change our driving behavior depending upon whether we know the driver that is in another car nearby us. Let's agree to this notion.

The aspect that we might have more heartburn about would be whether kinship is the deciding factor.

You might change your driving behavior when you see that your boss is driving in the car next to you. Presumably, you would be more deferential in your driving and if for example that driver wanted to get into your lane, I'd bet that you would readily let them cut into your lane of traffic. Or, suppose you see your next door neighbor driving their car and they are trying to come into the street as they backout of their driveway, you are likely to slow down and wait for them to proceed, perhaps more so than if you were driving down a street and suddenly someone was trying to backout of their driveway (someone you didn't know).

We'll establish then that your driving behavior can be impacted based on whom else is driving another car and for which you're driving and your car will in some manner interact with that other car.

I'm not suggesting you will always suddenly become a kinder and gentler driver to accommodate the other person. Imagine if your neighbor is someone you detest because they have let their dog roam onto your grass and repeatedly left a treasure for you, and that in spite of your complaining, the neighbor has kept this practice going. In that case, I am doubting that you would patiently wait for them to backout of their driveway. You might zoom past or maybe even try to come up with some sneaky means to get them to backout of the driveway improperly and wreck their car.

In each of these instances of you changing your driving behavior, I've purposely tried to structure the situation to involve a complete lack of actual direct communication per se between you and the other driver. In the case of you helping out your daughter, you did not prearrange to aid her in making the right turn, nor did you give her a call on her smartphone as she was driving and explained what you were going to do. Each of the situations so far have been undertaken without any direct communication between you and the other driver.

This allows us to revisit the plants. Are the plants communicating with each other about what to do? Does one plant tell the other one that it can spread its roots and that the plant will let this happen? As earlier mentioned, it might be the case that they "talk" with each other, perhaps via using chemical signaling or the use of light signaling.

The plants though don't necessarily need to communicate with each other directly, just as you were driving your car and did not communicate with the other drivers directly. I want to be careful how I phrase that aspect. Yes, you didn't call or speak with the other driver. You might though have communicated in other means.

Your behavior might have been your form of communication.

When your daughter was getting ready to make her right turn, suppose she looked in her rearview mirror and was trying to gauge the nature of the traffic behind her. She maybe already realized that this was a risky turn. She was examining the traffic behind her and might have opted to forego making the right turn, which could be a sensible action if she judged that the oncoming traffic might get confused and potentially ram into her car. Better to go around the block and enter into a different entrance than to chance getting hit or otherwise boxing up traffic.

Upon looking in her rearview mirror, she noticed that the car behind her was slowing down. What luck! The other car was apparently by coincidence going to create a kind of traffic buffer and she could take advantage of it, allowing her to safety make the right turn. She might not have had any clue that the other driver was intentionally trying to help out. No matter, the facts are the facts, and the buffer creation has allowed her to proceed with the right turn.

I'd claim that we have these situations continually during our driving efforts. We have situations arise, and at times another driver might be intentionally helping you out, while in other instances the other driver's behavior just so happens to help you out. You might not ever know what was in the mind of the other driver.

Sure, we sometimes get a hefty clue of what the other driver has in mind. The other day, I was pulling out of a mall and a car coming down the street came to a halt, the car flashed its headlights at me, and it was quite apparent that the driver was purposely acting to enable me to come out of the mall by blocking the lane for me. Was this a completely altruistic act? Does the driver deserve the courteous driver of the month award?

Yes and no. The other driver ended-up turning into the mall at the same place as I had exited, which I suppose you could suggest that the other driver wanted to get me and my car out of the way, allowing them to more easily turn into the mall. The aspect worked out in both our favors. You could argue that it was an altruistic act, or that it was a mutually beneficial act, or that it was selfishly intended for the other person and it just so happened that it aided me. Interpret it as you wish.

Our driving behavior can alter depending upon the other driver. If the other driver is someone that we know, this is a likely behavior changing factor. We might directly communicate with the other driver, or we might not. Our behavior alone might be our form of communication and no other kind of "direct" communication is undertaken.

We spontaneously collaborate with other drivers when we drive. There is not necessarily any prearranged agreement between one driver and another. There is a lot of discretion when you are driving a car. Of course, you are supposed to drive lawfully, but within the legal definitions for proper driving there is a great deal of latitude about driving.

Consider what is going to happen once we have true AI self-driving cars on our roadways.

First, realize that not all AI self-driving cars will be the same. I emphasize this due to the commonly false notion that all AI self-driving cars will be the same. When I give presentations at conferences, I often find that people assume that the AI of self-driving cars will be entirely the same AI, no matter who developed the AI and want kind of car you are driving.

Wrong!

Let's set the record straight. The AI of the self-driving car that is made by auto maker X or tech firm Y will be different from the AI of the self-driving car maker Z or Q. There is no underground secret agreement between these auto makers and tech firms. They are all pursuing the AI in their own proprietary ways. There might be some amount of open source in their AI systems, providing a bit of intersection, but otherwise each will be having its own idiosyncratic AI.

There is also no set standard that specifies exactly how the AI is supposed to be built and nor how it is supposed to act. Similar to how humans are able to have latitude when driving a car, this lack of any enforced specification means that the AI of each of the auto makers and tech firms can differ from that of the AI of each other in terms of how the AI drives a self-driving car.

You might readily have one AI system from say auto maker X that is a very cautious driving system. It avoids taking any chances while driving. Imagine the teenage novice driver that you sometimes get upset about when you get behind them. That could be the AI system of auto maker X, in the sense of exhibiting driving behaviors of a similar nature to the novice teenage driver.

Meanwhile, auto maker Y has gone a different path. For their AI, they decide to make it the type of driver that goes all out. It will readily be the first one to zip ahead when the light turns green at a stopped intersection. When it makes turns, they are always done with gusto. It exhibits completely different driving behaviors than does the AI system of auto maker X.

I realize you might object and claim that isn't it possible for auto maker X to potentially "copy" the driving behaviors that are being exhibited by auto maker Y's AI? Or, the other way around? Yes, it is. But, keep in mind that if you are trying to force both of their AI's to become the same, I wonder why you today tolerate the aspect that there are different kinds of cars that you can buy, some that are high-powered, some that are stylish, etc.

In essence, I am suggesting that we are likely to have AI systems for self-driving cars that abide by the legal elements of driving and yet differ in other driving behavior respects. It could be that each of these auto makers and tech firms eventually decide to "copy" each other and have the same set of identical driving behaviors, though I've questioned this notion and tried to explain why I believe that the "commoditization" of AI self-driving cars is unlikely to occur.

We are now finally ready herein to piece together all the pieces of this puzzle. What is the puzzle? The puzzle is that I am leading you toward those plants. Yep, we are back to the plants.

We are going to have AI self-driving cars on our roadways and I hope you now agree with me that those AI systems will differ, meaning that the AI driving behaviors will also differ.

Presumably, the AI self-driving cars of auto maker X will exhibit the same driving behaviors as those of the other AI self-driving cars of auto maker X, namely, there will be a kind of kinship. There, I said it, the word kinship has now arisen.

The AI of the auto maker X will be the same and drive the same way, and we could potentially even pick out of a line-up which AI is being used by a particular "anonymous" self-driving car.

How so? If we disguised a bunch of AI self-driving cars so that we could not recognize the car maker, and we put them into a test track someplace and had those true Level 5 AI self-driving cars drive around, I dare say that based on what they do, we could tell you whose AI it was.

I'll use my somewhat extreme example from my earlier point about auto maker X and auto maker Y. During a run in the test track, we observe that one of the self-driving cars is always being overly cautious. The other one tends to butt up against other cars and tries to jam itself into a lane. I think it would be relatively easy to guess that the cautious self-driving car was using the AI of auto maker X, while the more aggressive self-driving car was using the AI of auto maker Y.

Again, don't discard my claims due to the extremes of suggesting one is overly cautious and the other is overly risky. There are a lot of other capabilities that will differentiate one AI self-driving system from another in terms of driving behaviors. I am only using the extremes herein to illuminate my point.

On a related aspect, I've already predicted that the general public will eventually come to figure out the driving behaviors of the various AI systems. This will lead to humans trying to play "pranks" on those AI systems.

If you are trying to jaywalk, and if you know that the AI of auto maker X is overly cautious, you merely step into the street and know that the AI is going to immediately halt that self-driving car for you. On the other hand, maybe auto maker Y's AI is not so forgiving. This could lead to untoward actions by humans trying to play with the AI's and seemingly attempt to "outsmart" them, and we might have injuries and deaths because of it. Pranks aren't going to be a good idea, nonetheless I'm predicting it is exactly what will happen (likely leading to regulations against humans playing pranks, though I've argued we need to make the AI less susceptible to pranks).

We've now nearly got all the pieces of the puzzle in place.

With the auto maker X and its AI that exhibits some set of driving behaviors, and with the auto maker Y and its AI that exhibits some other set of driving behaviors, we now have the potential for a kind of kinship.

The AI of X might have been developed under the assumption that other self-driving cars that are also using the AI of X will act in certain driving ways.

For other self-driving cars and their variants of however they've done their AI, the auto maker X is assuming those other cars are being driven by however they are being driven. This implies that the non-X AI's are considered the same as human driving behaviors and whatever happens to appear while on the road is just how that driving is taking place.

Let's imagine that the auto maker X has made their AI to be this sweet and kindly self-driving driver. It comes along on a highway and detects that the car ahead of it wants to make a right turn into a shopping center. Since this AI is the nice-driver, it opts to slow down and create a traffic buffer for the other car that is turning into the shopping center.

But it might be that the auto maker X's AI does not always necessarily undertake that approach. Suppose the car ahead did not signal and did not provide any kind of in-advance indication that it was going to make that right turn. The AI of the self-driving car had no way to realize that it could help the other car. Therefore, the car ahead perhaps makes the right turn, doing so without any warning, and the AI of the self-driving car was unable to assist, not having had any means to gauge what might happen.

On the other hand, suppose that the auto maker X's AI, being as courteous as it is, if it was making the right turn, it would have turned on its turn signal well in-advance of the turn, and perhaps lightly touched its brakes, trying to convey to any cars behind it that it was wanting to make a right turn.

Revisit the scenario. Let's pretend we have the car making the right turn and it is a self-driving car by auto maker X and running their AI. Let's further pretend that the car behind it is also a self-driving car, and it perchance happens to be a self-driving car also by auto maker X and running their AI. The self-driving car making the right turn is courteous and forewarns traffic, and the car behind it is courteous and upon detecting that the right turn is desired the AI opts to aid in doing so.

Kinship!

You could argue that the AI of the two self-driving cars, being of the same "bloodline" and acting in the same driving behaviors, have aided each other. You might say they did so out of kinship of each other. It is akin to you driving your car behind your daughter and opting to aid her in making her right turn. Isn't love grand.

There wasn't any direct communication per se about this collaboration. It was merely predicated on their native behaviors. It could be like two plants of the same bloodline, each aiding the other, doing so not necessarily because they talked about it, but due to their inherent embodied natures that click with each other.

How's that for a plot twist!

We can now embellish the kinship aspects. I'll add communication into the equation.

AI self-driving cars are going to be outfitted with V2V (vehicle-to-vehicle) electronic communications. This will allow AI self-driving cars to communicate with each other. You might have an AI self-driving car driving down the road and it encounters debris. This AI self-driving car sends out a broadcast to alert any other nearby AI self-driving cars that there is debris in the roadway. The other AI self-driving cars that are nearby receive the message and they switch lanes to avoid coming upon and hitting the debris. Thank goodness for V2V.

Let's see how V2V comes to play in this kinship element.

The self-driving car trying to make the right turn into the shopping center could broadcast via V2V a message letting other nearby AI self-driving cars know that the right turn is coming up. The other AI self-driving cars would presumably receive the message and ascertain what they will do about it.

I'm sure that you are already assuming that of course the other AI's will all be courteous and upon this V2V notification slow down and make sure that the right turn can be made safely. Why do you believe that to be the case? Because you have fallen again into the trap that all AI's of the all different self-driving car makers will be the same. As mentioned, they won't be.

Perhaps auto maker Y's self-driving car happens to be behind the AI self-driving car of auto maker X that is trying to make the right turn. The AI of Y might decide to avoid the right turn situation entirely and instead switches lanes. That's perfectly legal. There was no legal requirement that the auto maker Y self-driving car has to perform a traffic buffer block for the right turning car. That's not written in stone someplace.

Therefore, the addition of communication does not necessarily take us out of the kinship mode. You could still claim that kinship will make a difference. It makes a difference because of the driving behaviors and how the AI of the same self-driving cars will be of the same "bloodline" and potentially therefore be more likely to play well together.

Auto maker X's family of self-driving cars are in a sense, a family. They have familial roots. This could result in them collaborating in a manner that they would not normally do with self-driving cars outside of their family. The auto maker Y's family is a different family. The differences between the family of X and family of Y can appear in the act of driving and performing driving tasks on the roadways.

The communications aspects can either further reinforce the family, or it could potentially allow other families to become more family-like with each other.

When the right-turning self-driving car sent out the V2V about wanting to make the right turn, it could have also asked the self-driving car behind it to please act as a traffic buffer. In that case, the other self-driving car might go against its "normal" or default tendencies and opt to serve as a traffic buffer. Of course, there is no requirement that the other self-driving car has to comply with the request. It might turn down the request and basically say, hey buddy, you are on your own there, good luck making the right turn.

The nature of how V2V is going to work is still being figured out. It is relatively easy to agree to the protocols about what kinds of messages will be sent out. Trying to also agree to the meaning of the messages and whether or not other self-driving cars and their AI need to abide by things like requests, well, it's a lot harder to settle those aspects.

Conclusion

I know that some readers might misinterpret my remarks and inappropriately commingle together this notion of kinship and bloodline as though I am suggesting that the AI of self-driving cars is going to be sentient.

It would almost be too easy to take that tack. If we said that AI will become sentient and it was therefore presumably like humans, I would guess that we'd all more easily accept the idea that they would therefore have kinship with each other.

I am not at all using the sentient get-out-of-jail free card, which is often used when you cannot otherwise find yourself out of an AI related pickle. You just toss down the freebie card and say that by magic the AI will become sentient.

In fact, I purposely walked you through the research about plants, doing so to shift you away from the sentience topic and avoid having to go there.

When you think about kinship for living animals and humans, it is immediately coated with the sentient topic. On the other hand, bringing up plants, well, it's a means to get away from the sentient thing and focus instead on more rudimentary aspects.

I believe it is a pretty evident open-and-shut case that the AI of one self-driving car maker is going to likely be a better "fit" in terms of driving behaviors with the self-driving cars of its own ilk.

I suppose an AI developer could go out of their way to make me wrong on that aspect, and purposely try to make their AI self-driving cars combative with their own kind.

Good luck on that. I doubt it's going to get you many brownie points.

We need to consider the ramifications of having different styles of self-driving car driving, meaning that the AI's will differ across the auto maker or tech firm making the AI.

Though they will all presumably be driving in a legal manner, there is a lot more to driving than just driving by the law. The latitude and how you act and react to other drivers, and what you do in various driving situations are based on driving behaviors.

During the time period when we will have AI self-driving cars mixing with human driven cars, the ante is increased because now you'll be faced with AI with other AI, or is it AI versus other AI, along with AI with humans and their driving, or is it AI versus humans and their driving.

We might get some amount of road rage by humans that don't like the driving behaviors of some of the AI's.

If you are intent on acting out toward an AI self-driving car, you'd better think twice, perhaps the AI developer planted a road rage reaction routine and you won't like what happens once you activate it. Hey, I wonder if I just planted that seed.

CHAPTER 5

MACHINE-CHILD
LEARNING
AND
AI SELF-DRIVING CARS

CHAPTER 5

MACHINE-CHILD

LEARNING

AND

AI SELF-DRIVING CARS

Did you play with blocks when you were a child? I'm guessing you probably did, or at least you have seen children playing with blocks. For children, it can be an enjoyable pastime and seemingly keep them busy. For parents, the blocks are a quick and easy diversion for occupying a child and the parents generally assume that the child will somehow be better off as a result of playing with the blocks.

If you study cognitive development, you likely know that block playing can be a significant means of formulating various key cognitive skills in children. In addition to the cognition aspects, the physical manipulation of the blocks will tend to aid the maturation of various body agility and coordination skills. There's also the commingling of the mind and the body in the sense that the child is not solely gaining cognitively and not solely gaining in physical movement but gaining in a synergistic way of the mind and the body working together.

There's a lot going on with the stacking of those blocks!

Lance B. Eliot

When my children were quite young, I watched in fascination as they played with blocks. It was as though you could see the gears turning in their heads as they would examine the blocks. Here's what I guessed was happening. What's this, a block that is all blue in color? This other block is all red in color. That's interesting and worthwhile to note as a difference. Say, this blue block is bigger than the red block. That's another interesting difference. I wonder if I can do anything with these blocks? I'll grab one and see if I can throw it. Oops, now I don't have the block near me anymore – make mental note, don't toss away a block because it won't be within your grasp anymore. And so on.

Consider for a moment how much a child can learn by simply playing with a small set of blocks.

They learn about the physics of objects, such as whether they are solid or not, whether an object is strong or squishable in being able to be compressed, heavy or lightweight to hold, graspable or too large to grab, etc. They learn about the colors of the blocks. Are they the same color, are they different colors, does the color have anything to do with the other properties of the block?

They learn about what they can do with blocks. I can try to put one on top of the other. That was fun, the red block is now stacked above the blue block. Oh no, the red block fell off the blue block. Why did that happen? Apparently, the red block was so much bigger than the blue block that the blue block could not serve as a pedestal for the larger block. Can I put the smaller block on top of the larger block? Can I shake the two blocks once I've stacked them and will they stay stacked?

What was most exciting for me was to then observe my kids as they were able to eventually begin to play with the blocks and yet did not necessarily need to touch or handle the blocks to do so.

96

It is one thing to reach out and handle a block, it's another to represent them in your mind and be able to "handle" them in a virtual sense. I would ask them to pretend in their minds that they were placing the blue block on top of the red block, and then ask them whether the blue block would be able to stay there or whether it would fall over.

That's a lot of thinking.

You also need to "disconnect" your motor skills for a moment to try and mull over the matter in your mind. As you know, whenever you are sleeping you seem to be able to disconnect your motor skills and not physically act out your dreams. Well, a child has to learn that they can imagine something in their minds and yet not necessarily need to engage their body in those thoughts. It takes a bit of doing to realize those are two different things, one being thoughts, the other being physical manifestations.

When they became more proficient in simple block-like tasks, I would increase the level of cognition needed. I might tell them that there are now three blocks, even though they only see two in front of them. This third block is orange in color. It is the same size and shape as the red block. I might then ask them whether I could stack the imaginary orange block on top of the blue block.

That's another leap in mental ability.

This involves not actually having a physical representation in front of you. You need to mentally conjure the notion of a block. I would do this at first with the other blocks present, making it a bit easier because they could look directly at the existing blocks and use though as a means to envision an imaginary block. I would later on take away the other blocks and do the same kind of pretend. This means they need to have in their minds the prior images of the blocks that they did actually see, along with now faking the aspect of having additional blocks that they cannot see and have never seen.

You might start-off by giving a child blocks that are the same shape, weight, size, colors, and so on. After they play with those, and presumably learn some initial aspects, you might switch things up and put out blocks that are different in size and weight. Then, use ones that differ in shape and colors. Then, put markings on the blocks such as an X and an O shape. Then, put stick-like drawings of a cat, a dog, and other animals. Then, put letters of the alphabet on the blocks.

The notion is that you are progressively graduating the child to more complex elements. You don't necessarily need to explain this to the child. You just give them blocks with increasingly complicated matters and have them figure things out. The variety also keeps the child engaged. If the child has the same blocks over and over, the odds are that eventually the joy of playing with the blocks will wane. By changing up the aspects of the blocks, it gets the child reengaged. It also presumably stimulates the nature of their learning and expands what they are learning.

You might want to keep this in mind the next time that you buy a set of blocks for your close friend's young child. You are not merely buying blocks for the child, you are providing a learning experience. It could be that those blocks that you gave to that child were the key ingredient to the child later going to a top tier college and graduating summa cum laude. Well, perhaps that's a bit of an overstatement about the learning power of those blocks, but you get the idea.

When I was a university professor teaching Computer Science (CS) classes and particularly for my AI classes, I would assign AI development programming homework and projects that involved the stacking and use of blocks. This is a handy way to have the CS students learn about the principles of AI.

At first, the programming assignment would consist of merely receiving simpleton commands about make-believe blocks and the program would need to respond with the state of the blocks after pretending to perform the commands. A command might be to pick-up a red block and stack it on top of a blue block. The program would need to then report what the state of the blocks was. In this case, the answer would be that the red block is now on top of the blue block, and the blue block is sitting on the table.

Once the students got a hang of that aspect, the next step was to increase the "cognition" required by their programs. Their software would need to deal with many blocks and deal with a wide variety of blocks. This would increase the set of commands and increase the complexity of keeping track of the state of the blocks.

I then opted to have them begin to turn their "cognition" only programs into dealing with a real-world of actual blocks. A room with a robotic arm had a set of blocks on a table. They had to give commands to the robotic arm about moving of the blocks. They also had a camera that provided visual images of the blocks. The students had to write code that would take in the images and use those images to figure out where the blocks were, and also what kind of instructions were needed to send to the robotic arm for movement to touch and move the blocks.

I'd usually have them write this in the AI languages of choice at the time, such as LISP or Prolog, and at first not allow them to use any open source libraries, forcing them to write most of everything from scratch. I figured it was good for them to know the details. After we got done with those aspects, I'd then allow them to use the open source libraries, which you can imagine came as a great relief for some, while others preferred to cling to their own code. That's another handy lesson for them too.

They would then add a Natural Language Processing (NLP) capability to their budding AI program. They were to assume that someone wanting to play with the blocks could enter in narrative that their program had to interpret. This was harder than forcing the user to enter strict commands. Instead of my entering that the command of put the red block on top of the blue block, I could enter something like take that one block and put it on top of the other block. Notice that I did not mention the block color. Their NLP would need to ascertain that the verbiage was ambiguous and therefore ask for more clarity from the user.

I'd start this with the narrative being in written form. After that was done, I'd then have them allow the user to enter their dialogue via written and in verbal oration. This got the students to deal with NLP in both modes. The ante was increased too by having the user be able to give a meandering dialogue that wasn't necessarily directly about the blocks. I might carry on a dialogue where I first talk about how my day is going, and then mention something about stacking a block. The NLP had to be able to parse the dialogue and figure out what was useful and what was not, at least for the task at hand.

All told, this was a handy way to introduce the students to various AI techniques and approaches.

The sad thing is that all of the work was essentially unusable toward other kinds of AI problems. Yes, the students themselves had learned key AI aspects and could write anew code for a different type of AI problem, and they could even potentially reuse aspects of what they had put together for the blocks world. But, what they could not do was say to their blocks world, hey you, I want you to now learn something entirely new.

Wouldn't it be great if you could develop an AI system that was a learning one, which could go beyond whatever particular domain aspect you crafted it for, and it would be able to learn something else entirely, leveraging what it already knew?

Let's return to the story about the children playing with blocks. I think we would all agree that the children are not merely learning about blocks. If they were "learning" like most of today's AI programs, they would only henceforth be able to use their blocks learnings to play with more blocks.

When my children went into our backyard to play, I noticed that they right away took various toys in the yard like a tricycle and a rocking horse and put one on top of the other. When I asked them about this, they reported that these were like the blocks. You could stack them on top of each other.

I asked them to look at the houses in our neighborhood. Could those be stacked on top of each other too, I asked? Yes, they said, though they also noted that it would be a rather arduous thing to do and that stacking them was not likely.

In essence, they learned not just about blocks, but also the nature of objects and the characteristics of objects, along with how to cope with objects.

Regrettably, the AI programs that my students wrote were pretty much one-time specific to the blocks domain. Those programs could not be unleashed to learn about other everyday things and leverage what they now "knew" about blocks.

This is one of the greatest issues and qualms about today's AI.

By-and-large, most AI development is being done as a tailoring to a particular domain and a specific problem in-hand. It makes them narrow. It makes them brittle. They lack any kind of common-sense reasoning. They are unable to extend themselves to other areas, even areas of a related nature.

Most of today's AI systems are each a one trick pony.

Today's AI systems cannot be self-applied to other domains and nor be expected to learn what to do.

Even the vaunted chess playing programs are pretty much dedicated to playing chess. They do not on their own have a capability to be presented with a different kind of game and reapply what they "know" about chess to the other game. It requires a significant amount of human AI-developer effort to rejigger such an AI system from one domain to another.

My children certainly were able to readily leverage their learnings of one domain into another. For example, I started them with checkers. When I got them to next start playing chess, they already understood aspects such as the placing game pieces on squares and the moving of pieces from one square to another, which they had learned from playing checkers. They knew all kinds of tactics and strategies of playing checkers, of which, they could reapply those to chess. I'm not saying checkers and chess are the same. I am saying that they learned about boardgame playing and could leverage it to learn a completely different boardgame.

And so we are currently facing a situation in AI of having to develop each new AI application and do so by significant and prolonged manual intervention by a human AI developer. There are some pretty wild projections that to develop all the different kinds of AI apps that people seem to want, you'd need to enlist millions upon millions of AI developers. That's just not practical.

It also seems to me to be a kind of tossing in the towel if you are merely going to hire AI developers, one after another, and try to create a globe that is filled with AI developers (heaven forbid!). One would hope that we aren't going to just be making AI systems that each are their own separate island. The larger vision would seem to be that we'd want AI systems that can learn on their own. In this manner, there aren't armies of AI developers needed.

In fact, there are some AI purists that suggest we are all right now being distracted by writing these one-off AI systems. Sure, it is fun, and you can make money, and you are solving an "immediate" problem that someone has stated. But the purists are worried that we are not confronting the bigger challenge, the learning challenge.

How can we make AI systems that can learn and do so far beyond whatever particular learning aspects that we started them with? That's what are focus should be, these purists insist.

Maybe we ought to be focusing on making an AI system that is like a child. This AI system begins with the rudiments that a human child has in terms of being able to learn. We then somehow mature that child and get it to become more like an adult in terms of cognitive capability. We could then presumably use this adult-like AI to then be applied to various domains.

Let's consider that you want to create an AI system for medical diagnosis purposes. Today, you would likely study what a trained and proficient medial specialist does when diagnosing something. You would then try to pattern your AI around that kind of cognition. You might gather up thousands of images of say cancer scans and use Machine Learning or Deep Learning to pattern match on those images. The resulting AI system appears to be able to do a "better" diagnosis than the human medical specialist, perhaps being more consistent in detecting cancers and so on.

Your aim seemed to be to target doing the task as proficiently or more so than an adult human. Some would say you went after the wrong target. You might be better off to have started with a "child" kind of AI system that you could mature and graduate toward doing this adult-like task.

This is the crux of the AI machine-child learning notion.

It is believed by some that we need to first figure out how to create a machine-child-like capability, of which, we could then use that as a basis for shaping and reshaping toward other tasks that we want to have performed. By leaping past this machine-child, you are never likely going to end-up with anything other than an "adult" single domain system that cannot be sufficiently leveraged towards other domains.

Now, I realize that some might recoil in horror. What, you want to replicate human intelligence by creating child-like AI? It seems like a science fiction novel. Humans create AI in a child-like manner. Humans then mess-up and the machine-child becomes a pissed-off AI adult that decides to turn on its "parents" and kills all of humanity. Yes, we all know about the dire predictions of the coming singularity.

I don't believe that's an apt way to portray this. If you've already bought into the idea that we are trying to create some kind of adult-like AI, what makes it so strange to instead focus on a child-like AI that can be progressed towards an adult-like AI? It would seem that you would at least be consistent and object to the adult-like AI, if you also were opposed to the machine-child idea.

What does this have to do with AI self-driving cars?

At the Cybernetic AI Self-Driving Car Institute, we are developing AI software for self-driving cars. One aspect that some AI purists are asking is whether or not the auto makers and tech firms are taking the right tactic to developing AI for self-driving cars, and perhaps the AI community ought to instead be taking a concerted AI machine-child approach.

Allow me to elaborate.

I'd like to first clarify and introduce the notion that there are varying levels of AI self-driving cars. The topmost level is considered Level 5. A Level 5 self-driving car is one that is being driven by the AI and there is no human driver involved. For the design of Level 5 self-driving cars, the auto makers are even removing the gas pedal, brake pedal, and steering wheel, since those are contraptions used by human drivers. The Level 5 self-driving car is not being driven by a human and nor is there an expectation that a human driver will be present in the self-driving car. It's all on the shoulders of the AI to drive the car.

For self-driving cars less than a Level 5, there must be a human driver present in the car. The human driver is currently considered the responsible party for the acts of the car. The AI and the human driver are co-sharing the driving task. In spite of this co-sharing, the human is supposed to remain fully immersed into the driving task and be ready at all times to perform the driving task. I've repeatedly warned about the dangers of this co-sharing arrangement and predicted it will produce many untoward results.

Let's focus herein on the true Level 5 self-driving car. Much of the comments apply to the less than Level 5 self-driving cars too, but the fully autonomous AI self-driving car will receive the most attention in this discussion.

Here's the usual steps involved in the AI driving task:

- Sensor data collection and interpretation

- Sensor fusion

- Virtual world model updating

- AI action planning

- Car controls command issuance

Another key aspect of AI self-driving cars is that they will be driving on our roadways in the midst of human driven cars too. There are some pundits of AI self-driving cars that continually refer to a utopian world in which there are only AI self-driving cars on the public roads. Currently there are about 250+ million conventional cars in the United States alone, and those cars are not going to magically disappear or become true Level 5 AI self-driving cars overnight.

Indeed, the use of human driven cars will last for many years, likely many decades, and the advent of AI self-driving cars will occur while there are still human driven cars on the roads. This is a crucial point since this means that the AI of self-driving cars needs to be able to contend with not just other AI self-driving cars, but also contend with human driven cars. It is easy to envision a simplistic and rather unrealistic world in which all AI self-driving cars are politely interacting with each other and being civil about roadway interactions. That's not what is going to be happening for the foreseeable future. AI self-driving cars and human driven cars will need to be able to cope with each other.

Returning to the AI machine-child notion, let's consider how AI self-driving cars are being developed and whether the AI purists have a sensible idea that perhaps the AI community is currently off-target of what should be taking place in this realm of AI.

Let's start by considering how humans learn to drive a car.

In most jurisdictions, the youngest that you can begin driving a car is around 16 to 17 years of age. There are some rare exceptions such as South Dakota allowing a driver at the age of 14. The basis generally for using the mid-teen to late-teens as a threshold point is the belief that the human has to be mentally and physically mature enough to take on the rather somber and serious nature of the driving task.

Your arms and legs need to reach the pedals and the steering wheel, and you need sufficient command over your body and limbs to appropriately work the driving controls. You need to have the cognitive capability to perform the driving task, which includes being able to detect the roadway surroundings, assess what the traffic conditions are, make reasoned decisions about the driving maneuvers, and carry out your driving action plan. You need to be responsible and take charge of the car. You need to know the laws about driving and be able to perform the driving task as abiding generally by those laws.

Could an even younger person possibly drive a car? Sure, you could likely drive a car at perhaps the age of ten. For farmers, it was not unusual to put to work a young person on a tractor. Of course, you can contend that driving a vehicle on a farm is not quite the same complexity as driving it while on a crowded freeway or in a packed inner-city location. In any case, there is nothing that necessarily precludes the possibility of being able to drive at a younger age. It all depends on the mental maturation and the physical maturation.

You could potentially remove or mitigate the physical requirements of being able to drive. With today's voice command systems, you don't necessarily need to use pedals for braking and accelerating and could instead use voice instructions to the vehicle instead.

You don't necessarily need a steering wheel and the use of arms and hands, since you could use a facial tracking system and aim the car by the use of your head or eyes.

You might suggest that these alternatives are not better than the traditional physical controls and that the usual physical controls are tried and true, which makes sense, but the point simply being that we could find a means to accommodate a human driver that has not reached a particular physical size and they could still drive a car.

The cognitive aspects are likely not so easily overcome in terms of being able to accommodate a younger and younger driver. Yes, with the advent of AI self-driving cars, there is less that the human driver needs to undertake in terms of the driving task. But do we want to have potentially a child that serves as the "last resort" human driver that is supposed to be ready to take the controls if the AI is unable to perform the driving task? I'd doubt that we would want this.

So perhaps we'd all settle on the notion that having a human driver be able to start toward driving at the age of their mid-teens is about right. We could try to push to an early age, though this seems like it is heightening the risks of untoward aspects during the driving task.

How does a human learn to drive a car?

I remember that with my children, they began by taking a class in how to drive. The class consisted of classroom work wherein they learned about the rules of the road and the laws that govern driving. They then got into a car and drove with a driving instructor, along with times that I went with them and coached or mentored them as they were learning to drive. The driving was initially in relatively save areas such as an empty mall parking lot. After this was used, the next step was a quiet neighborhood with little traffic, and then next was streets with a semblance of traffic, and then next was a harried freeway, and so on.

How are we getting AI systems to be able to drive a car?

It is rather unlike the way in which we get a human to learn to drive a car. The AI system is developed as though it is an adult driver and we then test it to see if it can perform as such. There is not particularly a learning curve per se that the AI itself has to go through. Yes, I realize that he Machine Learning (ML) and Deep Learning (DL) is undertaken, but it is done mainly for the capability of being able to detect the surroundings of the self-driving car, such as whether there are cars nearby or pedestrians in the street. The ML and DL is not similarly focused on learning the rules of the road and the laws of driving and other "cognitive" elements of driving a car, instead those tend to be baked into the AI system by the AI developers.

Here's now the point by some AI purists that pertains to this matter.

They would say that we should be trying to develop an AI system that has the capacity to learn, in the equivalent fashion somehow of what a human teenager does, and we should then use that foundation to essentially teach the machine-child to be able to drive a car. This would be equivalent to the human teenager learning to drive a car.

Notice that I am purposely saying "equivalent" because I want to separate the notion of the AI being the exact equal to a human versus it being of some equivalent nature. I don't want to get us stuck in this discussion on whether the AI is using the same biological kinds of cognitive mechanisms as a human. Some say that we'll never get a "thinking machine" unless we can precisely replicate the human brain in automation, while others contend that we don't necessarily need to crack the code of the brain and can instead construct something that is equivalent. I'm not going to get us bogged down in that debate herein and so please go along with my saying the word "equivalent" in this discussion.

You could suggest that we are currently doing a top-down approach to constructing the AI for self-driving cars and that this alternative is a bottoms-up approach. In this bottoms-up approach, you focus on creating a systems environment that has a capacity to learn, and you then put it toward learning the task at hand, which in this case is driving a car.

Would we be better off going in that direction as a means to achieve an AI system that can sufficiently drive a car that's the near same as a human that can drive a car?

It's hard to say. I think it is considered a much longer path due to the aspect that we don't yet know how to construct this kind of an open-ended learning AI system that could do this. In the classic race of the turtle versus the hare, the top-down approach gets us out-the-gate right away and shows progress, while the bottom-up approach is more like the hare that will plod along slowly.

There are some that assert that we aren't going to be able to achieve true Level 5 AI self-driving cars and we'll eventually hit the limits of this top-down approach. At that point, the world will be asking what happened. How come the vaunted true Level 5 was not achieved? If you were to say that it was because we started at the wrong place, it could be a bit disturbing.

The AI purists would say that the glamour of today's progress on AI self-driving cars is regrettably merely reinforcing the no-successful-end top-down approach. Yet, they would say this is a tease and confusing us all into not doing the true hard work of aiming at the bottom-up approach. Not only won't we get to the true Level 5, but the AI field overall will be hampered and not have made as much progress because we avoided the machine-child path.

Here's another twist on this topic that you might find of interest.

Maybe the AI purists are right and we need to focus on the AI as a learning system, crafting a machine-child, for which we then advance and progress and mature it into various kinds of adult-like AI systems.

If they are indeed right about this, what is the lowest "age" machine-child AI system that we should be trying to develop?

For the moment, in terms of driving a car, I suggested that we'd aim at a teenager machine-child cognitive level. That seems to fit with the cognitive maturation of when humans learn to drive a car. Perhaps though the teenage cognitive level is too old. We might need to aim at a younger cognitive maturity age.

We can revisit the blocks world. I had mentioned that children use blocks at a very young age and that the act of doing so is much more than simply playing with blocks. These quite young children are learning all kinds of aspects about the world overall. They are also learning to learn. They must gauge what they don't know and how they will learn it. This is a dovetailing of learning something while also learning about how to learn something.

Does it seem plausible for AI developers to construct an AI system that magically is at the teenage years of cognitive capability, or do we need to aim at a much younger age for the machine-child that we want to build? The human teenage cognitive skillset already includes the learnings of having played with blocks as a child. It could be that we can't leap past that when artificially creating such an AI system. This block playing as a baby or infant could be integral to being able to ultimately produce a machine-child that has the teenage cognitive capabilities.

I know it seems farfetched to consider that you might need to start at the baby or infant level and begin by having an AI system that plays with blocks. From blocks to driving a car? That seems not so related.

I'll offer a variant on the blocks world and see if it helps. Most children are likely to have had a tricycle or something similar when they were very young. You might have grown-up riding a Big Wheel, which is a famous kind of tricycle that is today listed in the National Toy Hall of Fame. For those of you that are nostalgic about the Big Wheel, you'll be pleased to know that there is an annual celebration that occurs in San Francisco on Easter Sunday's of people riding on Big Wheels. It is a BYOBW, Bring Your Own Big Wheel event!

Anyway, I bring up the topic of tricycles to offer something that might seem closer to the nature of driving a car.

I noticed that when my children were very young and rode their tricycles, they would at first bump into things as they rode the contraption and had to get used to being in motion while using the vehicle. They quickly figured out that they needed to steer the tricycle and avoid objects. They realized there were stationary objects that had to be avoided. They soon realized there were moving objects that had to be avoided, including other tricycle riders and "pedestrians" such as parents walking around as the children were riding. They had to mentally calculate the speeds, direction and distances of other objects and relate them to their own speed, direction and efforts of "driving" the tricycle.

The kids also learned that they at times needed to quickly hit the brakes on the tricycle to avoid hitting things or to be able to make other kinds of maneuvers. They realized or learned that they could accelerate via pumping their legs on the tricycle pedals, and the use of acceleration was vital to how they traversed an area. They made a mental map of the area in which they were riding and would try to optimize how to get around the backyard area and then out to the front yard area.

Does this sound familiar in terms of the kinds of cognitive and physical skills needed for being able to later on drive a car? I'd say so.

I know it is still a jump to go from riding a tricycle to being able to drive a car, but the point is that if you weren't sure how learning about blocks was related to driving a car, hopefully you can see that riding a tricycle is very much related to being able to drive a car. The tricycle riding leads to a set of cognitive and physical skills that can serve as a handy base when later on learning to drive a car.

Per the AI purists, we might need to focus on developing AI systems at the infant or baby cognitive level and get those AI systems to mature forward from that starting point.

When I mention this notion at AI conferences, there is usually someone that will say that this could lead to a kind of absurdity of logic. I seem to be suggesting that teenage age is too late, so we need to aim at infants or toddlers. But, maybe that's too late and we need to aim at a baby or even a newborn. But, maybe that's too late and we need to aim at conception.

At that juncture of the logic, we seem to have hit a wall in that it perhaps no longer makes sense to keep going earlier and earlier in the life cycle. And, if we can readily claim that jumping into the life cycle at any point will deny us the earlier learnings, it would seem that we have no choice but to start at the start and cannot merely pick-up the mantle at a later point such as a baby or infant.

Others would say that this is an absurdity of logic reduction and that we can get onto the life-cycle merry-go-round at a place that it is already spinning and still be fine. We don't need to reduce this to some zero point.

Let's pretend that we agree to shift attention of the AI community toward developing an AI machine-child system. We hope this will get us more robust adult-like AI systems. We especially hope that it will get us a true Level 5 AI self-driving car system, wherein we are using the AI machine-child to have it gradually become the equivalent of a licensed human driver.

There are other aspects about childhood of humans that we need to wonder whether they are essential to progressing the AI machine-child toward machine-adulthood.

For example, there is a period of time when a child will undergo so-called childhood amnesia. Usually around the age of 7, your memories of your younger days begin to rapidly erode. You seem to retain key learnings, but specifics of particular dates, events, and other aspects are gradually lost. No one yet knows why this takes place in humans.

One theory is that your brain is undergoing a radical restructuring and reorganization, which it cognitively needs to do to get ready for further advancements. It is perhaps akin to a house that was fine when you only had a few people living in it, but when you get toward twenty people the house needs to be overhauled. You need to knock out some walls and make space for what's going to come next. Maybe that's what happens in the brain of a toddler or young child.

Others say that you maybe don't lose any of your memories at all. They are all still there in your noggin. Perhaps the brain has merely put many of those thoughts under lock-and-key. The assumption is that you don't need them active and they can be archived. This is why at some later point in life you might suddenly have a flashback to a younger age, doing so because the lock-and-key was opened for that particular filed-away item.

In any case, if we build ourselves an AI machine-child that is at a young age of say 3 or 4 years old, cognitively as equated to a human, and if we progress forward the machine-child, will we eventually need it to undertake the childhood amnesia that humans seem to encounter?

Perhaps the AI machine-child won't need to do so. Or, maybe we don't do so and then the AI machine-child gets stuck and cannot get past the age of 7 in terms of cognitive maturation. Some would say you need to do likewise with the AI machine-child as you would with a human child, while others say that we don't necessarily need to replicate the same aspects as a human child and that we are carrying the metaphor or analogy of the machine-child too far.

The aspects of how to progress forward or mature the AI machine-child gets us into the same kind of bog. For example, a child does not just sit in a classroom all day and night and learn things. They wander around. They sleep. They eat. They daydream. They get angry. They get happy. The question arises whether those are all inextricably bound into the cognitive development.

If all of these other experiences are integral to the cognitive development, we then are faced with quite a dilemma about the AI machine-child.

Whereas we might have assumed we could build this AI cognitive machine and mature it purely in a cognitive way, perhaps we need to have it experience all of these other life related experiences to get the cognitive progression that we want.

I'm sure you've seen science fiction movies whereby they decide that they need to raise the AI robot as though it is a human child, aiming to give it the same kinds of human values and experiences that we have as humans.

Would we build the AI machine-child and then need to act like it is a foster child and adopt it into a human family? Also, if so, this implies that it would take years to progress the AI machine-child, since it is presumably taking the same life path as a human. Are we willing to wait years upon years for the AI machine-child to gradually develop into an adult-like AI?

I think you can see why few AI developers are pursuing this path and especially as it relates to AI self-driving cars. Imagine that you go the head of a major automotive firm and try to explain that rather than building an AI system today that will drive self-driving cars tomorrow, instead you are proposing to develop an AI machine-child which after maturing it for the next say 15 years it might be able to act as a teenager and you can train it to drive a car then.

Boom, drop the mic. That's what would happen. You'd get a startled look and then probably get summarily booted out of the executive suite.

For those of you intrigued by the AI machine-child approach, I'm guessing you might have already been noodling on another aspect of the matter, namely, whether there is any top-end limit to the cognitive maturing of the AI machine-child.

In essence, maybe we could keep maturing cognitively the AI machine-child and it would surpass human cognitive limits. It would just keep learning and learning and learning. This takes us to the super-intelligence AI debate. This also takes us into the debate about whether we are going to reach a point of singularity. Of course, you could maybe try to argue that if this machine-child is somehow the equivalent of humans, perhaps it does have an end-limit, as it seems humans do, and the machine-child will eventually reach a point of dementia.

Conclusion

I hope that when you next see a child playing with blocks or riding on their tricycle that you will admire all of the hidden learning and cognitive maturation that is taking place right in front of you, though it might not be evident per se since you cannot peek into their brains. Will we only be able to ultimately achieve true AI if we cannot replicate this same life-cycle of cognitive maturation?

If you believe that we are currently on an AI path to a dead-end, you might find of value the AI machine-child approach. In a sense, we might need to take two steps backward to go five steps forward. The steps forward at this time are maybe going to hit a brick wall. Instead, the AI machine-child might be the means to get past those barriers.

The topic of AI machine-child often gets chuckles from people and they toss off the topic as a crazy sci-fi kind of notion. They might be right. Or, they might be wrong. It's not so simple as making a handwave of claiming that the notion has no merits. Even if you don't buy into the notion entirely, there are bits and pieces of it that might be applied to our AI approach of today.

Excuse me for a moment, as I hear the AI machine-child crying in the crib, and I want to get over to it before the poor thing gets into a tizzy. A future car driver is on its way!

CHAPTER 6

BABY-ON-BOARD
AND
AI SELF-DRIVING CAR

CHAPTER 6

BABY-ON-BOARD

AND

AI SELF-DRIVING CAR

You've undoubtedly seen the famous Baby On Board signs that were a crazed one-hit wonder during the mid-1980s. When the fad first emerged, it seemed like these ubiquitous yellow-colored signs and their bumper sticker variants were popping up on cars everywhere. The moment that you pulled onto the street from your house, you'd likely see the Baby On Board prominently on the backs of cars streaming down your street, assuming you lived in an area that had young families that were eager to announce their baby occupant.

At first, it seemed that most people genuinely placed such a sign in the rear window of their cars as a means of letting other drivers know that there was a baby or small child inside the moving car. The notion was to forewarn other drivers to be especially careful when driving near to the car, presumably wanting to make sure that other drivers were supposed to regard the car as "special" since it contained a baby.

I remember that some drivers that didn't have children or had children that were far beyond the baby age were somewhat disturbed at the emergence of these signs. Did the sign imply that other drivers were callous around other cars and that by posting a Baby On Board sign they should clean-up their act? It was kind of a back-handed insult to these other drivers. One interpretation was that you, the person reading the sign, were a really crummy driver and that by announcing the presence of a baby, you were having a finger wagged at you to not be such a carefulness and witless driver.

There were some drivers that actually then became upset and decided to purposely drive recklessly near such a car, trying to show that other car who's the boss. The appearance of the Baby On Board sign became a kind of beacon for those affronted drivers. This might seem nutty now, but whenever a widespread fad like that emerges, there are bound to be some that don't like the fad and profess to make it backfire.

Rumors abounded that the sign was actually intended to alert emergency services or first responders whenever they came upon a car accident scene. If there was a wreck of cars, presumably the bright yellow sign would standout and the fire department responding would know to find a baby inside that particular car. Some assumed that there was apparently a high chance that your baby might get overlooked, and maybe you as an adult sized body would be dragged out of a decimated car, but your baby would get left behind.

The original developers and firm that brought the Baby On Board to worldwide attention had mainly in mind the idea of forewarning other drivers to be careful when near to a car with a baby in it. There is scant evidence to suggest that somehow babies weren't being pulled out of car wrecks. Nor was there evidence that once the signs became popular that somehow it raised the chances of a baby being discovered that was otherwise going to be overlooked in a demolished car.

For some people, the sign shifted in meaning toward a source of pride that they had a baby, regardless of whether the baby was actually in the car at the time or not. In other words, many people bought the signs and put them on their cars, doing so as a showcase that hey, I've got a baby, and congrats that I have one. You might not have normally been telling the world that you had a baby per se, but this sign made it easy to make such an announcement.

Of course, having the sign on your car when you didn't actually have your baby in the car was kind of defeating the purpose of the sign. If you were inclined to believe in the theory that the sign would give a crucial clue to first responders to look for a baby in a wrecked car, the sign was now at times going to endanger first responders by having them search in vain for a baby left behind. This would increase the risk for the first responders and quite adversely undermine the matter. It made things potentially worse rather than for the better.

This aspect of leaving the sign in your car window when you didn't have a baby in the car was yet another source of aggravation for some other drivers. Those drivers that were perturbed at the prevalence of cars using the sign and yet didn't have a baby in the car were at times tempted to look inside your car as you drove past. If they did not see evidence that a baby was in your car, these irked drivers would sometimes honk their horn at the car or try to perform untoward maneuvers nearby the offending car and its offending driver in a kind of retaliation. Take down your sign, some of them would exclaim in anger.

Another viewpoint about the baby in the car warnings was that it maybe was good for the driver of that car that had the baby, causing that driver to be more cautious in their driving. Allow me to explain. Suppose the driver of a car that had a baby in it was in front of you and suddenly cut you off in traffic. Well, that's a move that endangers the baby in that car. Some hoped that the people putting the sign onto their car would become more thoughtful drivers as a result of their own realization that they had a baby in their car. In that manner, the sign is really for the driver of the car that has the baby in it, more so than to alert other drivers about the car with the baby in it.

Eventually the Baby On Board signs became a kind of meme, akin to the nature that we have today on social media whenever something catches the fancy of the public at large. Parodies sprung up and it became popular to put a faked version on your own car window.

For example, there was the Baby Driving version, the Mother In-Law In Trunk version, and the Baby Carries No Cash version, and so on. Millions of the bona fide versions were sold and some estimates say that many millions more of the parody versions were sold.

Use of the sign on your car was considered questionable in other ways.

For example, some states in the United States got worried that the signs would use up space on your car window and obstruct your view. It was even outlawed with a ticketed violation in some jurisdictions, prohibiting you from putting one on your car window. Another concern was that the signs were distracting drivers and causing them to focus on reading the sign rather than watching the road and traffic conditions. Since the sign didn't seem to have much of a greater useful purpose per se, the distraction factor made it overly dangerous in comparison to whatever benefit it might provide.

There are various urban myths and other fascinating tales during the heyday of the Baby On Board signs. One popular tale was that drug smugglers would at times use the sign, in hopes of fooling the police into assuming that a car that had drugs would most certainly not have drugs, because of course no one would put illegal drugs into a car that had a cute innocent baby in it.

Partially due to the confusion about the sign and the backlash, the fad eventually waned. Nonetheless, the sign and the saying became on enduring icon. You would be hard pressed to find anyone that did not know about the Baby On Board signs in the sense that they've seen one either in real-life or seen it online someplace. The younger generation that did not grow-up with the signs have often heard about the signs or seen the signs and slogan portrayed in a variety of TV shows, movies, online games, and in a wide variety of other ways.

There are offshoots of the Baby On Board usage, such as wearing such a sign as woven into an apparel item worn by a pregnant woman. Some view this as a clever way to say a baby is on its way. There is a nostalgic side of the market too. You can still get the signs and put them onto your car, which you'll see from time-to-time on the roads. As usual, not everyone is keen on the use of the sign. There are some that say you are opening yourself to notifying prospective kidnappers or other hoodlums that might be interested in grabbing your baby, or that they can use the sign to strike up a conversation with you, acting as though they know you, and try to scam you in some other manner.

It's a cruel world out there.

Let's for the moment consider what it means to truly have a baby on-board of your car. Putting aside the matter of the famous sign, what kinds of things should people be doing if they actually are carrying a baby in their car. This might be especially instructive for those of you that have yet to drive a car with a baby in it.

Perhaps the most attention and discussions about having a baby inside a car involves the use of a baby seat for the child. Going all the way back to the 1920s, the early versions of baby car seats were essentially sawed-off high-chairs that had straps and some other restraints on them. The focus was to simply keep the baby from being able to move around in the car. There wasn't much thought given to the safety of the baby and nor what might happen to the baby when the car got into an accident or performed some radical driving maneuver.

Until the late 1960s, most baby seats were about the same in terms of lack of careful consideration for what a baby seat should do. The auto makers began to provide so-called love seats and guard seats for housing a baby inside a car during the latter part of the 1960s, and then during the 1970s the United States began regulating the safety aspects of baby seats.

At one point, there was almost a baby seats "war" in which different baby seat makers vied to get parents to buy their particular brand and models of baby seats. Do you have love in your heart for your baby? Would you give anything to protect your baby?

If so, it seemed that the baby seat makers would shame you into buying the most expensive baby seat they could make. The more the baby seat looked like an astronaut's seat, it was assumed by many parents that they were doing the right thing by buying such an elaborate contraption.

During this time period, there was research undertaken that indicated having the baby ride in the backseat is much safer than having the baby ride in the front seat. This seems rather intuitive in that you figure that any accident is likely to smash or cause flying debris to appear in the front seat, and so by placing the baby in the back seat you are essentially cocooning them further away from the mayhem.

There was also research that indicated the baby should be placed in a rear-seat facing manner. Thus, not only should the baby be in the back seat, the baby should also be facing toward the back of the car. You can imagine that some parents were dubious about this approach. How could they watch their baby and make sure the baby was okay during a driving journey? Which was more important, having the baby in the presumed proper position for a car crash, which might happen once in a blue moon, or have the baby facing forward such that via glancing back or looking the rear view mirror the parents could instantly see the status of the baby.

Another factor became how to affix the baby seat into the car. Sadly, many of the souped-up baby seats were difficult to install into the actual seat of a car, and thus some parents discovered to their dismay that though they spent a fortune on the baby seat, it did little good during a crash because the baby seat itself was not well affixed in the car. This led to a massive campaign to try and explain to parents how to install their baby seats. To this day, it remains a potential difficulty and concern.

The baby seat makers were able to realize that parents wanted not only a car baby seat but also wanted other kinds of seating for their baby. You might have a stroller that your baby sits in and have a separate car baby seat. If you went for a trip on a plane, you'd need to take your baby stroller and your separate baby seat too. Knowing how to use both of those completely incompatible contraptions and their idiosyncrasies made it more arduous to use them. This led to the all-in-one approach of devising baby seats that worked for cars and for strollers and for other purposes too.

Though the car-related baby seat topic tends to dominate attention about having a baby in a car, I'd like to cover various other elements involved in having a baby in car as well.

One aspect that I alluded to already involves the desire to keep tabs on the baby. An adult in the car should presumably be making sure that the baby is doing okay. This would usually involve trying to watch the baby and see how the baby is doing. You might also be listening to determine whether the baby is happy or maybe crying. The baby might also wiggle around and be flailing, the movement of which might make noise or might catch your visual attention out of the corner of your eye.

If you are driving a car and it is just you and the baby in the car, this desire to drive well and pay attention to the baby can be challenging.

It would be one thing too if the baby was seated adjacent to you in the front of the car, but the baby being in the backseat makes it even more arduous to keep tabs on the baby. I've seen many an adult that is transfixed on their rear-view mirror, trying to watch their baby, and angling the rear-view mirror downward rather than keeping it in position to see the cars behind them.

Sometimes the driver will repeatedly glance over their shoulder, turning their head away from the traffic ahead. This is another dangerous gambit, similar to trying to use the rear-view mirror to watch your baby. For each moment that you think you are doing the right thing by looking at your baby, you are likely increasing the chances of getting into a car accident. It's a tough balance. Do you not try to keep tabs on your baby and risk the baby somehow having troubles and you don't realize it, but in so doing you are maybe putting the baby into greater danger due to driver distraction?

Remember earlier about the Baby On Board signs and that some believed it was really supposed to be for purposes of getting the driver with the baby on-board to be safer? Part of the belief was based on the idea that drivers with a baby in their car are going to axiomatically be distracted and therefore be a worse driver. In fact, some of the other drivers that were irked at the drivers with babies in their cars was that those such drivers tend to often make late lane changes or do other acts that suggested they were distracted and only periodically watching the road.

Which is more important, your catching the drool coming from your babies' mouth, or making a proper lane change when going at 65 miles per hour freeway speeds? Trying to be a one-person band when driving a car is often quite arduous when you have a baby in the car. There you are, worrying about the baby, worrying about the traffic, and who knows what else might be on your mind. It's a lot to deal with as a driver.

If you have another adult in the car with you, hopefully the other adult will assume the duties of keeping tabs on the baby. That's the theory, though of course it can sometimes merely splinter the attention of the driver even further. The driver might be watching the other adult to make sure the adult is properly keeping tabs on the baby, and meanwhile the driver is trying to still on their own keep tabs on the baby. You've now got the driver contending with two living creatures at the same time. It's not always the case that this will lessen the distractions of the driver, but at least it provides the possibility.

Now that I've covered the aspects about the baby seat and the difficulties of keeping tabs on your baby while you are driving a car, let's consider some other elements too.

Suppose you put the baby into your proper baby seat and the baby seat is correctly secured in your car. Good so far. You opt to go on a leisurely drive along the coastline. It's a gorgeous sunny day. You drive along the coast highway and admire the ocean and the sunshine. Unfortunately, you failed to consider the sun exposure that the baby is getting in the backseat of the car. The baby is likely not able to realize the dangers of sun exposure and nor alert you to the aspect they are getting sunburned (as you know, adults get sunburned all the time, not realizing it is happening until long after it occurs).

This brings up the importance of making use of sunscreens, either physical ones on the car windows or attached to the baby seat, or some kind of protection for the baby from the sun rays. That's another element to be considered when you have a baby in your car.

Suppose you put the baby into the baby seat and have put the baby seat next to the rear window. A baby might be able to open the window and endanger themselves. Maybe even open the car door. This is the reason that many cars now have childproof locks on the rear windows and doors. This is yet another element to keep in mind about having a baby in the car.

Lots of other dangers are possible. You might accidentally close a window on a baby's appendage, or likewise close a door. You might leave the baby in the car and the baby could get injured or die from heat stroke.

While driving the car, if you take a turn or curve in a harsh manner, it could toss the baby around, in spite of the baby seat protection. The baby's limbs might not be conducive to sudden braking or sudden accelerations. There are some doting parents that perhaps become overly protective as drivers and they go exceedingly slow and take turns agonizingly sluggishly, which though you could say is the right kind of spirit, can actually increase the chances of getting into a car accident. Becoming a hazard on the roadway due to overly cautious driving can be a downfall for a loving parent.

The last point on this topic for now is that there is still that question about what happens to the baby when an emergency occurs.

As mentioned earlier, the Baby On Board sign was not especially adopted to deal with making sure that first responders would know to save a baby in a wrecked car. From a slightly different viewpoint, there is the matter of how a parent can best extricate their baby from a car if there is an emergency. Do you try to remove the baby from the car seat and then remove the baby from the car? Or, would it be more prudent to remove the entire baby seat with the baby in it? You might have only split seconds to decide what to do and therefore should have considered beforehand what you will do.

What does this have to do with AI self-driving cars?

At the Cybernetic AI Self-Driving Car Institute, we are developing AI software for self-driving cars. One important "edge" problem involves having the AI be of assistance when you have a baby inside the self-driving car.

Allow me to elaborate.

I'd like to first clarify and introduce the notion that there are varying levels of AI self-driving cars. The topmost level is considered Level 5. A Level 5 self-driving car is one that is being driven by the AI and there is no human driver involved. For the design of Level 5 self-driving cars, the auto makers are even removing the gas pedal, brake pedal, and steering wheel, since those are contraptions used by human drivers. The Level 5 self-driving car is not being driven by a human and nor is there an expectation that a human driver will be present in the self-driving car. It's all on the shoulders of the AI to drive the car.

For self-driving cars less than a Level 5, there must be a human driver present in the car. The human driver is currently considered the responsible party for the acts of the car. The AI and the human driver are co-sharing the driving task. In spite of this co-sharing, the human is supposed to remain fully immersed into the driving task and be ready at all times to perform the driving task. I've repeatedly warned about the dangers of this co-sharing arrangement and predicted it will produce many untoward results.

Let's focus herein on the true Level 5 self-driving car. Much of the comments apply to the less than Level 5 self-driving cars too, but the fully autonomous AI self-driving car will receive the most attention in this discussion.

Here's the usual steps involved in the AI driving task:

- Sensor data collection and interpretation
- Sensor fusion
- Virtual world model updating
- AI action planning
- Car controls command issuance

Another key aspect of AI self-driving cars is that they will be driving on our roadways in the midst of human driven cars too. There are some pundits of AI self-driving cars that continually refer to a utopian world in which there are only AI self-driving cars on the public roads. Currently there are about 250+ million conventional cars in the United States alone, and those cars are not going to magically disappear or become true Level 5 AI self-driving cars overnight.

Indeed, the use of human driven cars will last for many years, likely many decades, and the advent of AI self-driving cars will occur while there are still human driven cars on the roads. This is a crucial point since this means that the AI of self-driving cars needs to be able to contend with not just other AI self-driving cars, but also contend with human driven cars. It is easy to envision a simplistic and rather unrealistic world in which all AI self-driving cars are politely interacting with each other and being civil about roadway interactions. That's not what is going to be happening for the foreseeable future. AI self-driving cars and human driven cars will need to be able to cope with each other.

Returning to the topic of having a Baby On Board, let's consider how the AI can be of assistance if you do indeed have a baby inside of a self-driving car.

For an AI self-driving car that is less than a true Level 5, there should be a human driver in the car, and in that case the AI could potentially assist the driver in ways other than driving the car per se, such as monitoring the baby and relaying status of the baby to the human driver.

The AI could use the interior-facing cameras of the self-driving car to do facial recognition about the baby. Does the baby look okay, or is the baby turning blue because of swallowing something that might be blocking their airway passage? The emotional state of the baby can be potentially interpreted via the facial expressions and movement of the baby while in the baby seat. The self-driving car also will have an audio microphone inside the car that can be used to listen for sounds, including the baby crying or the baby cooing.

It is likely that the baby seat will have its own Internet of Things (IoT) devices such as detecting the heart rate of the baby and other vital signs, of which this data can be conveyed to the AI of the self-driving car. There is also a likelihood that the AI can ascertain whether the baby seat is properly secured within the self-driving car. This would be based on sensors within the seats of the self-driving car and also in combination with the camera images showing whether the baby seat is slipping around or staying in place.

The human driver would presumably be able to focus on the driving tasks expected of the human and would feel reassured that the AI is monitoring the status of their baby inside the car. The AI would be able to provide a verbal indication to the human driver about the status of the infant. This could be an interactive dialogue as based on the Natural Language Processing (NLP) capabilities of the AI system that are incorporated to engage the human in discussions about the driving task.

Beyond the simpler status aspects, the AI if specially developed with capabilities for assisting in baby monitoring would be able to detect some of the more potentially dangerous aspects that can befall the baby.

For example, if the baby is seated close to a car window, the AI via the visual image processing could detect if the baby tries to go outside of the window or tries to get the car door open. The AI could detect when the human driver opts to leave the car and hopefully therefore ascertain if the baby is being left behind in the car, reducing the chances of hot car deaths when an infant is inadvertently not removed from a car when needed. The AI might be able to detect sun exposure that the baby is getting and warn the human driver or possibly adjust the windows automatically to block the suns rays. And so on.

When an AI self-driving car gets involved in a car crash or other disabling action, if the AI system is still functioning it could act as a kind of Baby On Board alert capability. This could involve the AI system getting the car to perhaps honk its horn as a sign that there is a baby in the self-driving car (though this is obviously a dubious means and could be misunderstood). The self-driving car might have external e-billboards that the AI could use to display a message for first responders that indicates a baby is inside the car (assuming the e-billboards are still functioning).

The AI could use V2V (vehicle-to-vehicle) electronic communication to potentially send out a message indicating that a baby is inside the car, which might then get picked-up by responding vehicles and relayed to first responders. Likewise, the AI might use V2I (vehicle-to-infrastructure) electronic communications to inform a nearby element of roadway infrastructure and of which the first responders might also be in contact with the roadway edge computing devices.

Though I've emphasized these various communication means to inform others about a baby inside the car, I'd like to also mention that this same kind of messaging could be used to indicate more aspects beyond the notion of a baby being on-board the car. The AI could indicate how many occupants there are in the self-driving car. The AI might be able to ascertain the general medical status of the occupants, such as whether they are still breathing or not and how injured they are. The AI could provide the status of the car itself such as whether it is still running or if it is crumpled up.

All such information would be handy for emergency responders as they seek to get to the scene of the car accident.

So far, I've focused on the AI acting as a kind of assistant to the human driver that is present in the self-driving car and trying to be a nanny to watch over the baby.

Would this help ensure that the human driver remains more attentive to the driving task? In other words, if the human driver knows that the baby is being closely monitored and the AI is informing the driver about the status of the baby, perhaps the driver would no longer feel compelled to turn their head to look at the baby seated in the back seat or try to watch the baby via a rear-view mirror.

You could counter-argue that the AI attention might spur the human driver toward being less attentive to the driving task. For some drivers, perhaps they might normally glance at the baby on a periodic basis when unaided by the AI. If the AI is continually giving status updates, it could spark the human driver to become more aware of the baby and therefore divert their attention toward the baby more so. Of course, that's the opposite of what the AI monitoring is supposed to be achieving. A well devised AI monitoring system would presumably inspire confidence in the driver that the baby is being monitored sufficiently.

There is also the factor that the human driver is also likely being monitored by the AI. Whenever the human driver turns their head, the internal-facing camera would be able to detect this head turning. The AI would be able to gently caution the driver about diverting of their focus away from the driving task. In that sense, even if the human driver is somewhat inadvertently sparked to look at the baby, the AI can help the human driver to realize this is occurring.

One question that is a bit thorny involves what to do if the AI detects that something untoward is happening with the baby.

I remember when my children were babies and at one point, I had one of them in their baby seat in the backseat, and a passenger in the car turned to look and suddenly exclaimed "Oh my gosh!" as though something horrible had just happened.

This greatly startled me, and I assumed that somehow my offspring had gotten injured or was choking or something really bad was taking place.

Instead, it was simply that a toy had been ripped apart and the fluffy pieces were all floating around the backseat of the car. The passenger had reacted a bit over-the-top to this. There was no immediate danger involved. I didn't know that status at the instant of the exclamation and so I reacted rapidly by immediately pulling over to the side of the road. This was a dramatic car maneuver and not one that I would normally have made. After realizing that this was not a true emergency, I cautioned the passenger that in the future they ought to be more careful as to how they react to such circumstances and be thoughtful of the impact it could have on the car driver.

How should the AI convey a potential urgency to the human driver if the AI detects something is amiss about the baby? I doubt that we want the AI to make any loud exclamations or otherwise startle the human driver. The AI would need to balance between informing the human driver and not otherwise causing the human driver to make any sudden and untoward reactive actions.

Let's next consider what the AI can do about a baby being inside a self-driving car when the self-driving car is at a true Level 5.

Since the true Level 5 self-driving car does not need a human driver, this implies one of several possibilities about the baby being inside the self-driving car.

First, it could be that there is an adult in the self-driving car and essentially an occupant with the baby. In that case, the adult would hopefully be monitoring the baby. The AI could still be monitoring the baby, perhaps as a double-check or as further assistance to the adult. If the adult is perhaps weak in their faculties, maybe an elderly grandparent that is not so able to tend to the baby, the AI might serve as an adjunct to the adult.

Second, it could be that there is not an adult in the self-driving car and only a minor that accompanies the baby. This is an easy scenario to imagine. Suppose you decide to have your AI self-driving car drop-off your two children at grandma's house. You are too busy to go along. You put your 6-year-old daughter and your baby boy into the self-driving car, and you command the AI to take them to grandma's.

You are making an assumption that your 6-year-old daughter can take care of the baby during the driving journey. Though you might believe that to be the case, in most states you are likely violating a provision about making sure that an adult is accompanying your baby. A minor is not considered the equivalent of having an adult present.

I'm sure that people will be tempted to assume that with the AI monitoring the baby and their daughter, and with the likelihood too of the remote parent being able to electronically communicate with the AI self-driving car, such as watching the camera feeds, this will be sufficient to then allow their unaccompanied children to be driving around in the AI self-driving car. Parents that are pressed for time will consider this handy as a means of transporting their children for them.

I'd say that we are heading toward a societal, ethical, and regulatory matter that will require discussion and debate. Right now, if you do ridesharing for your children, they nonetheless still have an adult in the car, namely the ridesharing driver. There is in theory no means for you to currently put your underage children into a car and have that car go anyplace without at least one adult present, namely the human driver.

We can make the scenario of having underage occupants even more extreme. Suppose you put your baby into the baby seat of the AI self-driving car and then command the AI to take your baby over to the house of a babysitter that you use. During the driving journey, the baby is unaccompanied. There is no other human inside the self-driving car.

Should we be comfortable with the idea that if the AI is monitoring the baby and suppose that the parent has remote access, we are okay with the baby being in the car by itself? It seems hard to imagine that we would as a society accept this idea. If the baby suddenly has a severe problem, there is no immediate recovery possible since there is not another human inside the self-driving car.

You might try to claim that the AI self-driving car could try to seek help if the baby is having troubles. Maybe the AI dials 911. Maybe the AI sends out an emergency beacon via V2V and seeks assistance from other nearby cars and their potential human adult occupants. Perhaps the AI drives the self-driving car to the nearest hospital. Yes, these are all possibilities, but they seem rather second-best, at best, in terms of caring for the baby.

We'll have to wait and see what we opt to do as a society.

Let's pretend that the practice of having your baby in a true Level 5 AI self-driving car and alone as a human occupant gets outlawed. We all know that practices that are outlawed are not necessarily ergo no longer undertaken. A parent might opt to normally not put the baby in the AI self-driving car by itself, but perhaps they decide to break the rule, just this once, and do so because they are pressed to do something else and believe they have a good reason to violate this law.

What then? Well, we could guess that the AI would likely be able to ascertain that the baby is alone in the AI self-driving car. If that's the case, should the AI then refuse to proceed? Perhaps we have the auto makers and tech firms place a special stop-mode that the AI won't allow the self-driving car to get underway if there is a baby and no accompanying other human (this has its own challenges too, such as whether the other human is a minor versus an adult, etc.).

Or, suppose the AI self-driving car gets underway, somehow then realizes there is an unaccompanied baby in the car, should it report this aspect to the authorities?

Perhaps it calls the police. The AI could drive the self-driving car to the nearest police station or rendezvous with a police car. I realize this seems farfetched and hard to contemplate, but these scenarios are bound to happen.

If we eventually have hundreds of millions of AI self-driving cars on our roadways, all kinds of things are going to occur in terms of how people decide to make use of an AI self-driving car. Suppose too that you are a ridesharing firm and you are letting people use your Level 5 AI self-driving cars. A rider puts a baby into your ridesharing car, tells the AI to go to some destination, and slips out of the self-driving car. During the driving journey, something happens to the baby and it gets injured. Who is responsible for this? Since you provided the ridesharing car, presumably you have some culpability in whatever happens to the unaccompanied baby.

I've predicted that we might see a new kind of job role in society, namely the role of being a kind of AI self-driving car "nanny" or caregiver. The person would be hired to ride in an AI self-driving car and be there to accompany minors. They might also be there to aid someone that is elderly and not of full faculties. They might be there to assist in riders getting into and out of the AI self-driving car. Note that the person does not need to know how to drive a car (because the AI is doing the driving), which would reduce the barrier to entry for these kinds of positions. Etc.

Conclusion

As a final thought for now, let's assume that there is a baby inside an AI self-driving car, and the baby might or might not be accompanied by another human (as I say, this is yet to be decided by society).

Should the AI self-driving car drive any differently?

Some would assert that the AI should drive the self-driving car in a fully legal and cautious manner, regardless of who or what might be inside of the AI self-driving car. I think this is a bit of an over-simplification of the matter. There are degrees of driving that can range from being overly cautious to overly carefree. It is conceivable that the AI can devise a smoother ride for situations such as having a baby inside the AI self-driving car.

When my children were babies, I would definitely be more delicate when I saw a pothole up ahead or a dip in the road. If they had fallen asleep, I would try to avoid any radical turns or fast maneuvers. All of those driving aspects were perfectly legal and none of them were illegal. There is a wide range of discretion in how you drive a car, within the bounds of driving legally.

One aspect too will the possibility of trying to avoid car sickness for your baby. Adults can get car sick. Babies can also get car sick. I would suggest that a baby is maybe even more generally prone to potential car sickness. The manner of how you drive your car can contribute toward car sickness. In that sense, the AI could adjust its driving approach to try and reduce the chances of car sickness ensuing for a baby, if there is a baby inside the self-driving car.

Baby On Board. This kind of signage is a reminder that for AI self-driving cars, we need to consider the "special case" of what should be done when a baby is inside a self-driving car. We cannot ignore the matter. One of the more vexing issues will be whether a baby ought to be riding alone while inside a true AI self-driving car. The initial reaction would be that the baby should definitely not be alone, but this is something as a society that we have yet to fully address.

Would you want your AI self-driving car to announce that you do have a baby on-board of your self-driving car? We might see a resurgence of the fad. Via external e-billboards of the self-driving car you might announce it. You might have the V2V let other cars nearby know. Are you doing so for safety purposes or for the desire to brag or for what purpose? Or both? We might have a variant of these kinds of signs, one that says AI On-Board. That's something we ought to know about.

CHAPTER 7

COP CAR CHASES

AND

AI SELF-DRIVING CARS

CHAPTER 7

COP CAR CHASES

AND

AI SELF-DRIVING CARS

Most people have a New Year's resolution involving going on a diet or exercising more. Apparently, here in Los Angeles, making a resolution to lead a frantic car chase and be relentlessly pursued by the police is popular too. On January 3, just a few short days after our New Year's Day celebrations including the famous and breathtaking Tournament of Roses Parade, a seemingly crazed driver led the cops on a two-hour wanton driving romp throughout the Southern California area.

In this highly dangerous venture, the driver managed within a half-hour of the chase to ram into a person riding a scooter and after doing so continued the driving rampage. Notably, having later skidded into parked cars and after multiple attempts to be stopped by the police, the fleeing car began to look like something you would see at the end of a rather eviscerating demolition derby. The front windshield was shattered, and observers wondered whether the driver could now see the road ahead at all. The sides and front and rear of the car were all dented and various underbody parts of the vehicle were hanging loose or dragging or had fallen off.

You might not be aware that there is a well-known method often used by the authorities to try and curtail a chasing car, a method known as the PIT maneuver.

Most Californians have heard of the PIT maneuver since we are considered the capital of car chases in the United States. We seem to have more car chases than any other state. Last year, we had a reported 800 or so official car chases. To count as a true car chase, there must be a police car or highway patrol car that undertakes the chase. Once an formal car chase gets underway, the news media usually provides nonstop coverage and sends their helicopters that do freeway traffic updates over to the top of the chase for breathless reporting. We all seem to tune into our radios or TV's or live streaming to keep up with the chase and where it is going.

The letters of "PIT" are said to mean Pursuit Intervention Technique, or some say it means Pursuit Immobilization Technique, or maybe it means Precision Intervention Tactic, or some believe it is Push It Tough. This tricky maneuver involves a police car coming up alongside the fleeing car and then bumping into it, doing so to cause the target car to spinout. It is hoped that the spinout will then allow the police cars to surround and block the fleeing car from further movement.

When I have tourists here and a car chase ensues, I can potentially hoard over them the keen knowledge of what transpires in these car chases and watch as they often become mesmerized by the chase. They often falsely assume that the PIT maneuver will for sure end the car chase. It is not a guarantee of ending the car chase.

Indeed, what made this recent car chase especially notable was the fact that the police tried the PIT maneuver a near record of four times on this fleeing car. Each time, the car did a spinout, but each time the driver managed to regain control and drove off. Some falsely assume that the spinout will cause the target car to become disabled and unable to further move. That's not the case. The main notion is that the driver is supposed to become disoriented, momentarily, and the spinout will allow the police to then corner the suspect by then surrounding or encircling the stalled car with a circle of blocking police cars.

On the fourth PIT maneuver, the bumper came flying off and the rear window of the car became completely smashed up. Undeterred, the driver continued the romp. You might wonder how did the car chase eventually end? He ran out of gas. Yes, the driver took to the freeways and headed down south toward San Diego. He got maybe half-way there and ran out of gas on the freeway. Once his car came to a halt, the police cars surrounded him. The driver still resisted and so the canine unit was used to help encourage the driver to give up, which he finally did so.

Not all of our car chases are quite so spectacular. We have ones that are short-lived and by the time you hear about it taking place, the chase has ended. Enterprising entrepreneurs have kindly provided smartphone apps that will alert you when a car chase gets going and can point you to local online coverage, allowing you to hopefully not miss a moment of the car chase excitement.

There are some locals that say the only reason they care about the car chases is to make sure they don't inadvertently get embroiled into one that perchance occurs when they are also on the road. By keeping tabs on where the car chase is going, you can try to reroute away from the path of the chase. Others are perhaps more forthcoming and openly state that they relish watching the car chases and believe it to be some of the best free entertainment around. For those of you that are historians, you'll likely recall one of the most famous car chases ever, the O.J. Simpson chase, which was a slow chase that weaved throughout the SoCal environs and drew huge crowds in-person and was watched in awe by people globally via broadcast TV.

According to various statistics about police-pursued car chases, the average nationwide chase only goes for about 3 miles. I'd wager that here in SoCal we tend towards longer car chases. Part of the reason entails our fine weather and the sprawling roadway infrastructure. It is perhaps easier to draw out a car chase here than it might be in other parts of the country, and we offer year-round weather befitting a robust car chase. We also are a car-centric location and tend to use our cars more so than might be occurring in other locales.

I often get asked why the police don't just fully ram the fleeing cars. The PIT maneuver is a bumping procedure and it is not the same as actually ramming a car, and so this begs the question why not indeed do a full ram instead? Well, you need to consider the risks to the police in undertaking a true ramming action. Trying to ram directly a speeding car is a dicey proposition. Yes, you might stop the fleeing car, but you might also cause injury or maybe even death to the police undertaking the ramming.

In fact, one of the aspects about car chases that makes it so dangerous is the possibility that the fleeing car might ram into the police, or might ram into other cars, or ram into pedestrians, or as in this recent case ram into someone on a bike or scooter. There can be a variety of untoward results during a car chase.

You might be somewhat surprised or perplexed to know that sometimes a car driver that has nothing to do with the chase will intervene when it gets near them, trying to aid the police by blocking the fleeing car. The police say don't do that. Leave the car chase to them and avoid getting involved in the car chase. These eager vigilantes think they are doing a grand thing by aiding the authorities. Though perhaps well-intended, it is not welcomed and in fact you could get in trouble for intervening.

There is an ongoing debate about whether the police should even pursue a fleeing car at all. Maybe it is safer to let the crazed driver get away. Why risk everyone else during the car chase? Doesn't the act of chasing the suspect lead to the driver being outrageously reckless and making dangerous driving maneuvers? If you let the driver go, they presumably would resume normal everyday driving practices and thus the risks to others on-the-road is lessened.

The counter-argument involves the idea that you are letting get away a potentially violent criminal that might be willing to break the laws in other even worse ways. Suppose the wanted driver later on opts to harm someone, perhaps killing someone? If you were a loved one that had a close relative or friend harmed by that criminal, you would certainly bellow that had the police fully chased and caught the culprit, the subsequent crime would not have been committed. Don't let dangerous people get away, would be the mantra there.

It is a delicate balance. Go after a driver and incur the risk that someone during the car chase will be harmed, versus letting the driver get away, but maybe they will later commit a dastardly crime. Some assert that if you routinely let a fleeing driver get away, you'll encourage more car chases, since the crooks will know that you aren't going to try and stop them. This seems to encourage illegal behavior, rather than discouraging it. If you always pursue the driver and make sure they get caught, it would seem to send a message that might actually curtail the number of car chases.

There are car chases that do not end in the driver being actually apprehended. I think that's part of the excitement for those that watch the car chases. Besides seeing what kind of wild car driving the person does, there is also the fascination about whether the person will actually succeed in getting away. It is almost always the case that the police end-up with the getaway car, but once the car comes to a halt, and if the driver and its occupants jump out and scatter, they are sometimes able to avoid arrest.

We had another recent car chase in which the occupants leapt out of the fleeing car, doing so during the car chase. They hoped to get away by presumably making the police choose between continuing to follow the car or having to stop to try and get them. If that was their logic, it wasn't very well thought out. These car chases often involve dozens of police cars in pursuit. Thus, the police usually have ample resources to then continue the car pursuit and also have some police that stop to go after the fleeing occupants.

Another question often posed asks whether the car chase could be undertaken entirely by helicopter. Just have a police helicopter that follows the fleeing car. The car driver might not even realize the helicopter is tracking them. In that case, there isn't a car chase per se underway and the driver might drive in a normal safer manner. The police helicopter can radio the police on the ground to keep them attuned to where the driver is, and once the car stops, the police can surprise the driver by suddenly appearing and apprehending them.

This is a nice idea, but it often falls apart in practical terms. There are places that you could drive into or under and for which the helicopter cannot readily follow. Once inside those places, like say a multi-level parking structure, the driver is likely to be able to get away on foot, doing so prior to the time that the helicopter can alert the ground forces to try and get the crook.

There are though many jurisdictions that do require the police to weigh a multitude of factors before giving chase via cars. If the driver is not believed to be armed and dangerous, and if the car chase was sparked by something rather benign, such as expired tags on the license plate, the police might opt to follow only via helicopter, doing so knowing that it increases the risk that the driver will maybe get away scot free. If the expired tags turn out to show that the car was actually stolen, and since this is a more serious crime, the police might deduce that this is someone of an inherently dangerous nature and so the risks of a full car chase are warranted.

Most of the car chases usually involve male drivers. It seems that the chances of a female driver undertaking a car chase is less common. I'm not making any gender-related remarks about why this is the case, and only pointing out that statistically the odds are higher that the fleeing driver is a male rather than a female. There was a police chase involving a female driver and for which she had originally been sought because she rolled through a stop sign, which is considered a low-level or relatively benign "criminal" act. The police then ran a background check via the plates of the car and discovered that she had no prior criminal record. They decided to abandon the car chase and instead waited at her home, which she eventually returned to, and she was arrested there.

There is more to car chase than meets the eye.

If the police are able to guess where the fleeing car is headed, there is a chance of setting up a roadblock to try and halt the car. Another alternative to a roadblock involves laying down a spike strip, which is a means of potentially ripping up the tires of the car as it runs over the metal spikes, which then will hopefully disable the car from driving much further. There are other inventive approaches such as one that casts a kind of metal mesh net over the fleeing car. These are techniques that have their own advantages and disadvantages, thus it is not necessarily the case that they are a foolproof way to successfully end a car chase.

A crucial part of the equation involves trying to ascertain the risks to humans. There is the risk of injury or death to innocents that have nothing to do with the car chase, other than perchance being in the wrong place at the wrong time. There is the risk of injury or death to the police involved in the car chase. We need to also include the risk of injury or death to the driver of the fleeing car and its occupants, if any.

You cannot assume that the occupants in the fleeing car are necessarily criminals. They might be carjacked or kidnapped. I mention this because there have been car chases involving cars with multiple occupants, and I've had some tourists that said the police ought to just force the car off-the-road and maybe it crashes or rolls over. This is chancy since you don't know the nature and status of the occupants, and you cannot risk tossing the baby out with the bath water, so to speak.

Plus, as much as you might detest the driver of the fleeing car, you cannot just summarily decide that the driver should be killed to stop the car chase. I say this because I've had some tourists that ask why not just have the police car pull alongside the fleeing car and have a police officer shoot their gun at point blank range and kill the driver. Wouldn't that end the car chase?

I suppose it would end the car chase. Of course, the fleeing car is for sure going to do something even wilder once the suspect is dead and still behind the wheel, but putting that aside, I don't think we can ask the police to render such outright killings. We do have a due process of law here.

The counter-argument by some is that the fleeing driver is putting others in danger and it is as though they have drawn a gun and are pointing it at the public, and so wouldn't a criminal pointing such a gun by eligible to be shot by the police? The argument seems perhaps persuasive, since the multi-ton car is a kind of weapon, but no, our society has not made the logical leap that this is the equivalent to carrying around and threatening people akin to wielding a gun.

Other aspects that you might not notice about a car chase involve the police doing other subtle but important actions to try and reduce the chances of someone getting hurt.

For example, the police that are following the fleeing car are typically a few yards back of the car, rather than being directly at the bumper of the car. This is thought to reduce the sense of pressure on the wild driver and hopefully will calm them and avoid the high speed and chancier kinds of chases.

The police will usually have their sirens on and be trying to warn other traffic that something is afoot. If other car drivers are paying attention to the normal aspects of driving, and even if unaware of a chase taking place, they will hopefully hear or see the sirens and flashing lights of the police cars and will pull over as expected. The police will sometimes also try to get ahead of the fleeing car and block intersections, and otherwise try to ensure that other drivers and pedestrians stay away from the underway car chase.

There's another tricky element you need to consider. Suppose the driver or the occupants have a gun or other weapons in the car with them. I mention this aspect because it also explains why the police want to stay a bit of distance away from the fleeing car. At any moment, the driver or its occupants could opt to open fire and shoot at the police. That's dangerous for the police and obviously part of the goal of these chases is to try and reduce the chances of the police getting harmed, in addition to protecting the general public.

What does this have to do with AI self-driving cars?

At the Cybernetic AI Self-Driving Car Institute, we are developing AI software for self-driving cars. One aspect to consider involves the potential of a car chase that in one means or another might involve an AI self-driving car and thus the AI ought to be ready for this to occur.

Allow me to elaborate.

I'd like to first clarify and introduce the notion that there are varying levels of AI self-driving cars. The topmost level is considered Level 5. A Level 5 self-driving car is one that is being driven by the AI and there is no human driver involved. For the design of Level 5 self-driving cars, the auto makers are even removing the gas pedal, brake pedal, and steering wheel, since those are contraptions used by human drivers. The Level 5 self-driving car is not being driven by a human and nor is there an expectation that a human driver will be present in the self-driving car. It's all on the shoulders of the AI to drive the car.

For self-driving cars less than a Level 5, there must be a human driver present in the car. The human driver is currently considered the responsible party for the acts of the car. The AI and the human driver are co-sharing the driving task. In spite of this co-sharing, the human is supposed to remain fully immersed into the driving task and be ready at all times to perform the driving task. I've repeatedly warned about the dangers of this co-sharing arrangement and predicted it will produce many untoward results.

Let's focus herein on the true Level 5 self-driving car. Much of the comments apply to the less than Level 5 self-driving cars too, but the fully autonomous AI self-driving car will receive the most attention in this discussion.

Here's the usual steps involved in the AI driving task:

- Sensor data collection and interpretation
- Sensor fusion
- Virtual world model updating
- AI action planning
- Car controls command issuance

Another key aspect of AI self-driving cars is that they will be driving on our roadways in the midst of human driven cars too. There are some pundits of AI self-driving cars that continually refer to a utopian world in which there are only AI self-driving cars on the public roads. Currently there are about 250+ million conventional cars in the United States alone, and those cars are not going to magically disappear or become true Level 5 AI self-driving cars overnight.

Indeed, the use of human driven cars will last for many years, likely many decades, and the advent of AI self-driving cars will occur while there are still human driven cars on the roads. This is a crucial point since this means that the AI of self-driving cars needs to be able to contend with not just other AI self-driving cars, but also contend with human driven cars. It is easy to envision a simplistic and rather unrealistic world in which all AI self-driving cars are politely interacting with each other and being civil about roadway interactions. That's not what is going to be happening for the foreseeable future. AI self-driving cars and human driven cars will need to be able to cope with each other.

Returning to the topic of police pursuits and car chases, let's consider how an AI self-driving car might get involved.

Before I offer some real-world aspects, I'd like to tackle the Utopian crowd that says we'll never have car chases once we have AI self-driving cars. In their view, it is pointless to talk about car chases since they won't ever happen. Why bother to consider something that you know won't occur?

Well, this presupposes that we have only AI self-driving cars on our roadways. As I've already mentioned herein, the day in which we have only AI self-driving cars and no legacy cars is a long way off in the future. We don't even know for sure that such a day will arrive. Perhaps society might not relent to having only AI self-driving cars on our roadways and insist that legacy cars can still exist. Or, maybe we aren't able to achieve true AI self-driving cars and continue to muddle along with human drivers, albeit those human drivers being augmented by some pretty slick advanced automation driving capabilities.

So, I will concede that if we someday had only AI self-driving cars, true ones, and if you are saying that as a society we would have the auto makers and tech firms ensure that there was some kind of "virtual spike strip" that would prevent an AI self-driving car from engaging in a car chase, I suppose we would not have car chases.

This though also has some weak points in that you could indeed have a car chase that gets started, but for which it would then presumably be easier to curtail. There is a chance of a carjacking, or some refer to it as a robojacking when involving an AI self-driving car. There is also the chance of a security breech that allows for someone to overtake the built-in controls of the AI and make it engage in a car chase. There is the change too of a bug in the AI system that would allow it to undertake a car chase.

My point being that the Utopian world still has to consider that there are various "edge" cases in which a car chase might still take place. I suppose if you are viewing the Utopian world as an all-perfect place, you might wave a magic wand and say that no human will ever do any carjackings, and that AI self-driving cars will never be vulnerable to a hack, etc. I wonder if this Utopian world also has candy and chocolates that flow out of the taps of our drinking fountains?

I think that covers the make-believe Utopian world and so now let's focus on the real-world.

We'll start with the notion that an AI self-driving car might become an innocent that gets inadvertently enmeshed into a car chase. Suppose we have a legacy car being driven by a human that is being pursued by human driven police cars. I had mentioned earlier that the police cars usually turn on their sirens and flashing lights, in hopes of warning other drivers to stay clear of the car chase.

Imagine that the AI self-driving car is driving along on some city street, quietly making its way to some destination, and all of a sudden it happens to come in contact with a police car chase that is underway. What will the AI do?

You might say that the AI should have already heard the siren or seen the flashing lights of the police cars. Yes, I agree that a well-designed and developed AI self-driving car should be able to detect the police car aspects. The visual sensors of the AI self-driving car will hopefully have detected the flashing lights and the sensor fusion will report to the virtual world model that there is a potential police car in an emergency mode. The AI Action Planner should then consider what to do, presumably pulling the self-driving car to the side of the road, or maybe rerouting the self-driving car away from the police car.

In terms of actually hearing the police siren, I've been advocating that AI self-driving cars need to have an audio listening capability, which most do not yet have.

As humans, we use our ears to listen for sounds that warn us about various driving related matters. You might hear the crunch of two cars hitting each other, being able to hear the sound before you can actually see where the accident has occurred. You might be listening and hear your own car make a sharp banging noise, which maybe means you've hit a piece of debris that you otherwise did not see on the roadway. Or, you might hear a police or fire department or ambulance siren, doing so before you can actually see it.

The omission of an audio listening capability is a significant detriment to driving a car, I assert. We humans use our sight and our hears to help us safely and successfully drive a car. The AI sensors of the self-driving car need to have a listening feature and need to incorporate this into the overall AI aspects of driving the car. I realize that some will say that by adding an audio feature, you are going to have AI self-driving cars capturing sounds all the time, and this could be a privacy invasion.

Though I certainly well understand the aspect that this use of an audio feature can be a privacy issue, I usually point out that with the other sensors that are already on an AI self-driving car you have presumably accepted the potential for various kinds of privacy loses.

The cameras on the AI self-driving car are capturing images and video of whatever is happening around the self-driving car, doing so pretty much all the time that the self-driving car is underway. That's a huge privacy question right there.

I am not trying to minimize the privacy question about the audio capture, and only pointing out that we have a much larger overarching privacy consideration about all of the sensory capabilities of the AI self-driving car, and thus the audio portion is but one added element.

Another means for the AI self-driving car to potentially become aware of the car chase would be via V2V (vehicle-to-vehicle) electronic communications.

The police cars might be electronically broadcasting a message via V2V to warn other nearby cars to stay away or be wary of the approaching car chase. In that case, the AI of the self-driving car might receive the V2V, and without yet seeing the police cars or hearing them, be forewarned about taking protective action.

I suppose that it might not even be the police cars alone that are broadcasting the V2V warning and it might be other AI self-driving cars doing so too. Imagine that for whatever reason the police cars are not yet broadcasting the V2V warning, and an AI self-driving car happens to detect the presence of the police car via its sirens or flashing lights, the AI might broadcast via V2V a warning to other nearby AI self-driving cars.

Here's a question I sometimes get. Suppose the car being chased opts to broadcast via V2V that all other cars should get out of the way? Could that happen? Yes, it could, and there might be legitimate reasons other than a car chase that such a message might be broadcast. This also brings up the conundrum that just because an AI self-driving car receives a V2V does not ergo mean that it is valid and something to immediately act upon. Dealing with V2V is going to be trickier than that (unless you live in the all-rosy Utopian world).

Another question is whether the car being chased might exploit the AI self-driving cars by sending out a V2V that gets those AI systems to actually put their self-driving cars into the path of say the police and thus block the police on behalf of the car being chased. Could that happen? Once again, the answer is yes, and it further highlights that just because a message is received it does not mean that the AI should at face-value believe it or nor act on it without first trying to validate or verify the matter.

Besides V2V, a warning about a car chase could occur potentially via V2I (vehicle-to-infrastructure) electronic communication. We're heading toward an era in which our roadway infrastructure will be "smart" and outfitted with all kinds of electronic gadgets. Suppose an intersection has a "smart" camera that detects a car chase that is upcoming. It might send out a flash message via V2I to warn other cars that the intersection is about to become a dangerous spot and stay away.

Okay, one way or another, we have some means for an AI self-driving car to be tipped to the aspect that a car chase is underway. This is handy and hopefully will allow the AI to try and prepare for the matter, either getting off the road or taking some other path entirely.

Should an AI self-driving car only attempt to stay out of the battle, or should it try to engage in the battle? Right now, as mentioned earlier, the police take the stance that the innocents such as other cars and their drivers are supposed to say out of the matter. Will this same policy continue when we have some smattering of AI self-driving cars? Don't know.

It could be that society opts to consider using AI self-driving cars as a helper in these car chases. It could be that the police via V2V are able to essentially "commandeer" your self-driving car and get the AI to use it as a pawn in the car chase. Maybe the police route a bunch of AI self-driving cars into a street to block the traffic and try and prevent the fleeing car from having any viable place to go.

Admittedly, it seems hard to imagine that as a society we would be willing to have "innocents" dragged into a car chase like this. I think that people are going to already have suspicions that the government is going to act like Big Brother and potentially take over our cars. This kind of ability to allow the police or any such authority to take over our cars, well, it seems hard to believe the public will stand for it. You might argue that if AI self-driving cars are mainly used for ridesharing, it could be that the government regulates that any ridesharing self-driving car must comply with the authority taking it over, but that's also likely to cause some angst by the public.

Here's another twist for you – what about the PIT maneuvers?

I've mentioned that the police can try to spinout a car by using the PIT maneuver. Should all AI self-driving cars know how to do a PIT maneuver? If so, perhaps the police or other authorities could commandeer an AI self-driving car and have it do the PIT maneuver on a human driven car that is being chased.

This is not overly farfetched. Suppose the police have an AI self-driving car and opt to make sure there are no humans riding inside of it. They then direct the AI self-driving car to go ahead and execute a PIT maneuver on a fleeing car being driven by a human. This means that no police officer needs to actually do the PIT maneuver and spares the human police officer from possibly getting injured while trying to do the maneuver.

Notice that I asked the question by posing whether "all" AI self-driving cars should know how to do a PIT maneuver. You might argue that only some AI self-driving cars should have such a capability. Note that it is essentially a software-only aspect in that you do not necessarily need any special gadgetry on the car to do the PIT maneuver. It certainly helps if the car doing the PIT maneuver has good bumpers and some other stuff on it, but it is not a necessity.

Some would say that perhaps the PIT maneuver software routine would be something only provided on certain kinds of AI self-driving cars, or maybe downloaded only when needed, using an OTA (Over-The-Air) updating to load the routine into the on-board AI system.

I'll add a twist to the twist. You can potentially defeat a PIT maneuver if you know how to cleverly drive when being approached by a car that wants to do a PIT maneuver on your car. I doubt many criminals know how to try and prevent a PIT maneuver from working. Anyway, suppose the AI knew how to try and curtail the likelihood of the PIT maneuver from being successful. Should the AI have that kind of capability?

These kinds of questions all raise various societal and ethics related kinds of points. We are heading to a time when the AI can potentially be made to do these types of things, such as being able to perform a PIT maneuver and/or potentially avoid being impacted by a PIT maneuver. The technology is going to allow these kinds of capabilities. It won't be a tech question and instead more of a societal question as to whether or not these kinds of capabilities are going to be allowed or not, and if not then how to prevent them from being put in place; while if they are allowed, under what circumstances will they be permitted to be employed.

I've now covered some of the rudiments about a car chase involving a human driven fleeing car and it being chased by human driven police cars and considered how an AI self-driving car might get enmeshed into the matter.

There is the chance of a human driven police car that gives chase toward an AI self-driving car. As I've suggested earlier, the Utopian world says this should never need to be the case. There should never apparently be a possibility of an AI self-driving car that needs to be chased.

Suppose I instruct my AI self-driving car to rush me to the pier. I'll for the moment make the assumption that the AI is going to drive the car only at the proper speed limit and it will not try to drive radically or go above the speed limit. I'm not saying that will be the case, and indeed have argued in my writing and speeches that we are going to have AI self-driving cars that don't drive with such strict adherence. Anyway, let's put that other argument aside for the moment.

The police find out that there's hostage in the self-driving car and so the police opt to follow. We are now having a car chase. If you think that all car chases involve going only at high speeds, you'd be wrong. There are many car chases that we see here in Los Angeles that are low-speed or slow speed pursuits. Believe it or not, there have been times that the driver obeyed all traffic rules and stopped at stop signs and never went faster than the posted speed limit, nonetheless it was a police pursuit.

You might argue that there's no need for the police to follow the AI self-driving car. For example, the police could maybe via V2V ask the AI where the self-driving car is going, and merely then have the police assemble there. Or, maybe the police use the OTA of the self-driving car and can find out where it is headed. Or, the police transmit a message to the self-driving car to tell the AI to stop the car, or maybe even have the AI drive the self-driving car to the police station, placing it right into the laps of the police.

Yes, those are all possibilities. But, suppose the AI self-driving car is currently incommunicado. It might be out of the range of electronic communications, or it might have the electronic communications being blocked by the driver that is using the AI self-driving car to flee. I'm sure that once we have a prevalence of AI self-driving cars, there will be all kinds of tips posted online about how to try and block the electronic communications features of your AI self-driving car (getting it to become an autonomous car that is not connected to the cloud or any other device).

In the case of no viable means to electronically communicate with the AI self-driving car, it would seem that the car chase is still on.

There might be some kind of other signaling that is agreed to be allowed to perhaps stop an AI self-driving car. Maybe the police show a poster board with a special code on it, and this gets the cameras to realize that the AI self-driving car should come to a halt. You can imagine though that this method has holes in it and could allow for anyone to potentially do the same to your AI self-driving car.

The police might resort to a driving tactic based on known driving behaviors of the AI self-driving car. For example, if the AI self-driving car is doing a simpleton follow-the-leader driving technique, perhaps the police car could get in front of the being chased car and gradually slow down the police car, which the AI might also then slow down as it would when following any car ahead of it that is slowing down.

There recently was the case of a Tesla driver that apparently was asleep at the wheel, and a highway patrol car got in front of the Tesla and was able to slow down and get the Tesla to also slow down. This was done until the car had been brought to a halt.

I am doubtful that this kind of pied piper approach is going to necessarily work on true AI self-driving cars. It is my hope that true AI self-driving cars will be much more capable. I've mentioned many times the dangers involved in people potentially "pranking" AI self-driving cars, doing so by knowing what the AI self-driving car is going to do, and my assumption is that future true AI self-driving cars will not permit this kind of pranking.

There are various other twists and turns in the circumstance of an AI self-driving car that might be leading a car chase.

For example, perhaps the auto makers and tech firms will include a capability of the AI to realize that it is actually leading a car chase.

This is somewhat tricky and involves detecting other traffic, but in any case, it is something that a human driver would be able to determine and therefore I claim that the AI ought to be able to do the same (since presumably for a true AI self-driving car the AI can drive in whatever manner a human could).

The AI, once it ascertained that it was leading a car chase, might then engage the human occupants in a Natural Language Processing (NLP) dialogue to discuss the matter with them. The AI might try using the V2V, V2I, and OTA to connect with the outside world and find out what might be occurring. The AI might have some kind of fallback posture that if it detects it is involved in a car chase that maybe it automatically pulls to the side of the road or takes some other pre-staged precautionary act.

The other variant of the car chasing would involve the police car itself being an AI self-driving car. Will we be asking police to drive cars themselves, when we presumably have a world of AI self-driving cars, or will we instead have the police be occupants or passengers in an AI self-driving police car?

Some would say that the AI is not going to be able to be the designated driver for a police car because the AI would not be able to drive in the same manner as trained police officers can drive a car, such as being able to make radical maneuvers and drive urgently when needed.

I don't quite get the logic of those that take such a position. Are they suggesting that the best the AI can do is the average everyday kind of driving? Though that's the first point of entry for AI self-driving cars, I don't know why things would stop there. It makes a great deal of sense that the AI would be able to drive in the same manner as a highly trained emergency driver could.

You might even make the case that we might be safer by having the AI drive those emergency vehicles.

If you believe that the reason that we have car crashes today involves various human foibles, those human foibles can likewise happen to a trained police officer or ambulance driver or fire truck driver. I'd say we ought to be aiming to have AI self-driving capabilities that can drive at the utmost of human driving. This would imply that then all AI self-driving cars have the "best" possible driving capabilities. Plus, the AI would presumably be connected with the V2V and V2I and be able to rapidly respond to real-time changes in the traffic and roadway, which a human driver might be less likely to be able to so respond.

Using AI swarm techniques, an entire set of police cars could coordinate and act together when undertaking a car chase. On a more macroscopic scale, we presumably could have AI self-driving police cars, AI self-driving ambulances, AI self-driving fire trucks, and any other kind of emergency responding vehicles that would all make use of AI for doing the driving. Whether as a society we'll accept this approach is a different question, and I'm merely suggesting that it would seem that we eventually would have the AI capability to do this, assuming we can achieve true AI self-driving cars.

Conclusion

Car chases. We watch them in rapt attention. What will happen? Will the driver get away? Will the police capture the culprit? Will there be problems during the car chase? What is the driver thinking? How will the police strive to stop the driver? And so on.

We are going to continue having car chases, until we reach the magical Utopian world that some postulate will occur. There are going to be AI self-driving cars on our roadways that might get inadvertently dragged into a car chase that involves a human driver chase car and human driven police cars, and the AI needs to know how to detect it, avoid it if possible, or escape it if needed.

I've also claimed that we'll potentially have car chases that are led by an AI self-driving car. This seems utterly counter-intuitive to most people and they shake their head in disbelief that it could ever happen. I hope that I've made a convincing case that it could happen. We need to be wary of it occurring and try to embody into the AI of the self-driving cars a capability to detect it and try to deal with it, if it comes to play.

We ultimately will likely have AI self-driving police cars, along with other emergency vehicles being driven by AI. I'm claiming that those AI self-driving police cars should be versed in undertaking a car chase, since they might be needed to do so when chasing a human driving a legacy car, or perhaps even when chasing an AI self-driving car.

For the foreseeable future, we are still going to have car chases. Whether you react to this assertion with fascination or horror, either way I'd say that we need to boost the AI of self-driving cars to have specific capabilities dealing with car chases. Putting our heads in the sand and pretending that the AI will never need to cope with a car chase is not a viable approach to the matter.

Hey, I just heard about an exciting car chase happening down the street, so excuse me while I go and take a look. Can't miss a really good car chase.

CHAPTER 8
ONE-SHOT LEARNING
AND
AI SELF-DRIVING CARS

CHAPTER 8

ONE-SHOT LEARNING
AND
AI SELF-DRIVING CARS

When my children were about kindergarten age, I told them about the mammal known as a platypus. I verbally described that it has fur, has webbed feet like an otter, lives mainly in the water, has the tail of a beaver, it has a snout like a duck, and they would be unlikely to spot one here in California. From my description, I'm sure they were dubious that such a creature actually existed since it seemed like a descriptive mishmash of other animals that they were familiar with, and perhaps I was trying to pull a fast one on them (I had told them earlier about grunion and after numerous grunion hunts, we had yet to see one!).

A few months later, we went on vacation to a zoo and the moment we came upon an actual pen of platypodes, I was pleasantly surprised that the children immediately pointed at and exclaimed that we were witnessing a set of real platypuses in-person. I had not prompted them to be considering finding any platypuses at the zoo. I had not mentioned anything at all about any platypus beyond my 15-second description that I had casually mentioned to them, off-hand, while we were driving home from school one day those several months earlier.

Smart kids, I reasoned.

Let me give you another example of their genius (proud father, you betcha!).

We had coyotes that were sometimes near where we lived, and the children had seen them from time-to-time at a nearby open preserve. There was even one occasion whereby a coyote dared to come into the local community of homes and wandered throughout the neighborhood late one night. This created quite a stir and there was an impetus by the community leaders to establish ways to try and keep the coyote and any wandering brethren from coming in.

After my children had seen coyotes in and around our neighborhood and become accustomed to seeing these creatures, one day I showed the kids a textbook picture of a coyote and I also showed them a textbook picture of a wolf. I offered no verbal explanation of the similarities and differences between a coyote and a wolf. I let them observe the picture for themselves. I merely pointed out to them that there are coyotes, which they had already seen with their actual eyes, and there are wolves (we didn't have any wolves nearby where we lived, thankfully).

You likely know that wolves tend to have round ears, while coyote tend to have taller pointed ears. Wolves tend to be larger than coyotes. There the differences start to get less distinguishable, since the fur of both types of animals is quite similar and in many other physical ways they appear very much the same. I could have mentioned that wolves tend to howl while coyotes tend to make a yapping sound, but in this case, I merely silently showed them a picture of the two types of animals.

Fast forward to a trip to the local snow-capped mountains, where we would go to try and get some skiing in (note, the city of Los Angeles itself gets no snow and thus if you want to ski outdoors, you need to go up to the local mountains, which is about a 2 hour drive or so; on some days, you can go surfing in the morning at the beach and then get up to the mountains to go skiing for the afternoon).

We were walking through the thick snow and suddenly a wolf came out of the woods and stood in front of us, maybe 20 yards away. It was surprising that the wolf would appear like this, since there were usually a lot of humans wandering around in this area. But we had stayed late, and it was getting dark, plus we were the only humans left in this particular spot, so perhaps the wolf felt like it was not in any particular risk or danger of making an appearance. I wasn't sure what the intentions of the wolf were. It certainly startled me and took my breath away as I tried to decide what to do next.

Meanwhile, the kids both whispered "wolf" and they knew this was a dangerous predicament. I was somewhat surprised they had not said "coyote," since we were generally used to seeing coyotes and it probably should have been the closest match to what we were now seeing in front of us.

Of course, they were right that it was a wolf. We waited a few moments and fortunately the wolf retreated back into the woods. I skedaddled out of there with the kids in rapid tow.

Why do I tell these two stories?

In the case of the wolf, the children had seen coyotes and so knew what a coyote looked like. I had shown them one picture of a wolf. From that one picture, they were able to identify a wolf when they saw one during our snowy adventure. You might say this is an example of one-shot learning. They had learned about wolves by merely having seen one picture of a wolf.

In the case of the platypuses, they had not seen any picture of a platypus and I had merely provided a verbal description. Yet, when seeing platypodes at the zoo, they right away recognized them. You might say this is an example of zero-shot learning. They had not seen any example of a platypus, thus they had zero visual examples to extrapolate from, but had used the description to be able to match what they saw at the zoo to the definition of the animal.

In traditional machine learning of today, most of the time we need to make use of thousands and upon thousands of examples of something to be able to train a Deep Neural Network or Deep Learning system on the item of interest. If you want to train an image processing system about platypuses via current Machine Learning (ML) techniques, you would gather up many thousands of pictures of platypuses and feed them into the system you had setup. Likewise, if you wanted to train the ML or DL on what wolves look like, you would need thousands of pictures of wolves.

When I say thousands, it could take hundreds of thousands of such pictures to try and get a solid matching capability of the ML or DL. This also would take a fair amount of computer processing time to undertake. You'd also want to have screened the pictures to make sure you are feeding the right kinds of pictures into the system. If you are feeding pictures of platypuses that also have say alligators in them, and if you aren't carefully scrutinizing the ML or DL, it could end-up mathematically conjure up a notion that a "platypus" can look like a platypus or like an alligator.

That won't do you much good when trying to find platypus somewhere inside a picture that you later feed into the trained ML or DL system. Sure, it might identify platypuses, but if there happens to also be an alligator in any of those pictures, the ML or DL might falsely report that another platypus has been found in the picture that you submitted.

In fact, one of the dangers about blindly feeding inputs into a DL or ML during its training is that it might pattern match onto aspects that you did not intend to be included. There is a famous story of the pictures of military tanks that were fed into a DL or ML system. Some of the pictures were of United States tanks and some of the pictures were of Russian tanks.

At first, after the training was seemingly completed, the DL or ML could readily discern other test pictures of U.S. tanks and Russian tanks. The researchers thought they had finished the job. Turns out that the pictures of the U.S. tanks were pristine photos, while the Russian tanks were mainly grainy photos. The ML or DL had considered the background and overall look of the photos as part of the pattern matching effort, doing so in a mathematical way. Thus, if it was shown pictures of a Russian tank that was in a pristine photo, the DL or ML would sometimes classify it as a U.S. tank. Similarly, if it was shown a picture of a U.S. tank that was in a cloudy kind of photo, the DL or ML would sometimes mistake it as a Russian tank.

In any case, the point is that to train today's DL or ML systems, you typically need to assemble a whole bunch of examples. This can be arduous to do. It can be costly to do. You need to make sure that the examples are representative of what you are trying to train for. You need to make sure that there is nothing extraneous that can potentially throw-off the pattern matching. You need to run the DL or ML for many iterations and chew-up lots of computer processing cycles, which can be costly. You then need to try and verify that what the pattern matching has found is something sensible.

Suppose instead that you could show a DL or ML an example based on just one picture. Imagine how easy it would be to then train the DL or ML. Here's a picture of a wolf. Via that one picture alone, it would be great if the DL or ML was then essentially done being trained. With one-shot learning, you had avoided having to collect thousands of examples and dealing with all the other troubles of doing the training.

Maybe you don't even have a photo of what you are trying to train the DL or ML on. Wouldn't it be great if you could somehow just describe what you are wanting to have the DL or ML pattern toward, and henceforth it could find that for you. This would be akin to my description of a platypus, from which the children were able to discern them when they actually saw it in-person.

You have now been introduced to one of the most vexing problems facing today's Machine Learning and Deep Learning. Namely, if humans can learn something by a one-shot or by a zero-shot, why can't we get ML or DL systems to do the same?

It is said that children by the age of 6 have supposedly around 1 x 10^4 number of categories of objects that they know about.

Based on these categories, when they are provided with something new, the children seem to cognitively be able to model on it, even without having to see thousands of whatever the item is.

Think about it.

Have you seen children sitting quietly and studying thousands upon thousands of photos of elephants to be able to figure out what an elephant most likely looks like?

I don't think so.

And yet that's what we are doing today to train the ML and DL systems that are being used in all kinds of ways.

There are some that suggest a one-shot can be flexible and that if you can do something in just a handful of examples it is about the same as doing so in one example only.

Therefore, they lump those few-shots into a one-shot.

They justify this by pointing out that they are not stretching the one-shot to be say a hundred examples or a thousand examples. Maybe a half-dozen or a dozen, they suggest, makes it pretty much the same as a one-shot.

I'll be a bit of a stickler herein and suggest that one-shot should literally mean one shot.

I'd like offer that we can use these ways of depicting the aspects of Machine Learning in terms of the number of "shots" or examples that are needed:

- Zero Shot Learning (ZSL) = there are no learning exemplars used per se

- One-Shot Learning (OSL) = one exemplar is used to learn from

- Few-Shots Learning (FSL) = more than one exemplar is used for learning and some number less than a number like maybe ten exemplars or a dozen or so

- Many-Shots Learning (MSL) = more than the FSL, let's say tens to perhaps hundreds to thousands of exemplars

- Mega-Many Shots Learning (MMSL) = more than MSL, let' say many thousands and possibly millions of exemplars

The desire would be to try and always aim at the least number of exemplars that might be needed to do Machine Learning, which makes sense because the more exemplars you might need then the generally the greater the effort and cost involved in finding the exemplars, preparing the exemplars, and otherwise undertaking the whole ML process.

If possible, we'd like to minimize the effort/cost to arrive at the needed ML.

Is it going to be always possible to find a means to get the number of exemplars down to the zero (ZSL), 1 (OSL), or few (FSL) categories of shot learning? Maybe yes, maybe no.

Cognitive development studies of children tend to suggest that how words are learned via sounds involves babies hearing hundreds and thousands of words and sentences that are spoken to them or near to them. When you talk to a baby, even though you might assume the baby is not "understanding" what you are saying, it is actually pattern matching your spoken sounds.

When you speak aloud a sentence, there are short gaps of silence between your words, and another slightly longer gap of silence between your sentences. You are so accustomed to these gaps that you don't even realize they exist. Babies hearing your spoken utterances are noting these silence gaps and garnering a kind of pattern matching about the nature of the spoken word. They grasp that words are shorter, and sentences are longer, and that sentences can have some number of these shorter sounding things in them.

I remember when my children were first born, people would speak to them in baby-talk, such as cooing at the them and saying nonsense sounds like baa-baa and boo-boo. Supposedly, these kinds of sounds are not going to help the baby formulate the kinds of "learning" best needed to understand true spoken language. You are making up some strange and out-of-sorts kind of nonsense language, which doesn't do them much good, and you instead should speak to the baby in normal adult language, which allows the baby to then begin to learn true spoken language.

The point being that it would appear that to formulate an understanding of spoken language seems to require a budding mind to hear hundreds and likely thousands upon thousands of exemplars of spoken words and sentences. Can this be reduced to just 0, 1, or a few exemplars? It seems unlikely.

One aspect that we also need to keep in mind is the nature of the learning outcome.

Let's consider my wolf example earlier. The kids said that the animal we saw in the snowy woods was a wolf. They got this right. Does this imply they learned what a wolf looks like? It is a bit overly generous to say so, because they might have just been wildly guessing.

Maybe they had no idea of the differences between a coyote and a wolf. Instead, they might have somehow else labeled this creature that came out of the woods as a wolf.

We'll also use the platypus example. I assumed that the children had mentally calculated that the creature we were seeing at the zoo had the requisite features of the otter's webbed feet, the beaver's tail, and the duck's snout. Suppose instead the kids used solely the duck's snout-like feature to label the animal as being a platypus. This is not going to be handy for future circumstances of them encountering other kinds of animals that also have a snout-like feature, for which my children might decide to call those as platypuses too.

Maybe if I were to have shown the kids pictures of platypuses, they might have landed on realizing that all three of the features were needed (webbed feet, snout, beaver's tail). Could I have achieved this with just one such picture of a platypus? Or, would have I needed a few such pictures? Or, would I have needed hundreds or thousands of pictures?

The crux is that we want to try and minimize the number of exemplars used for Machine Learning, but the question arises as to whether we can get the same kind of learning outcomes by doing so. If you are able to get the ML system to "learn" based on one exemplar, such as a picture of a wolf, but if the learnt result is narrow and unlikely to be robust enough for our needs, the learning itself has been insufficient and the minimal number of exemplars hasn't really aided our learning hopes.

Does this imply that the more the exemplars, the better off you will be? Suppose we line-up a dataset of a million pictures of dogs. All kinds of dogs. Big dogs, small dogs. Dogs that are happy, dogs that are sad. Dogs running, dogs walking, dogs sleeping. We feed these pictures into a Machine Learning system that we've setup.

After doing the training, we test the ML by feeding it some pictures of dogs that it had not been trained on. Let's assume the ML reports that those are pictures of dogs. Great! Meanwhile, we decide to also now feed a few pictures of cats into the ML system. It reports that they are dogs! What's this, a cat being mistaken for being a dog? The global union of cats will protest in droves, as they don't want to be miscast as dogs.

It could be that the ML opted to identify that any four-legged creature was a dog. Thus, when it received the pictures of some cats, after having done the training on the million dog pictures, it found that the cats had four legs and therefore reported they were dogs. Easy peasy.

Using tons of training exemplars does not guarantee us the kind of learning outcomes that we might be desirous of reaching. Presumably, the more exemplars the better you will be in terms of potentially getting good learning outcomes, but it is not axiomatic that larger datasets means that you'll get more robust learning outcomes.

There's something else we need to factor into the Machine Learning aspects, namely time.

Have you ever done one of those "Escape The Room" challenges? You go into a locked room and need to find your way out. The first time you do so, the odds are that you might at first be confused as to what to do. How are you supposed to find your way out? If you've never done one before, you might be completely bewildered as to what to do and where to even start to find a way out.

Upon seeing someone else in the room that opts to look for clues, you likely realize that you too need to try and find clues. You are a fast learner! Yes, you went from being utterly baffled to the realization that there are clues hidden in the room and you must find the clues, from which you can then potentially find a way out of the room.

In this case you were time-boxed in that the room escape is usually timed and you only have a limited amount of time to find the clues and ferret out how to escape. There is the time needed to actually discover the clues, decipher them, and then use those clues to escape. There is also the time needed to "learn" how to cope with being inside an escape room and learning how to proceed to escape it.

Upon seeing an exemplar of the other person in the escape room that was feverishly looking for a clue, you quickly learned how to play the game. Sometimes we might sit in classrooms for weeks or months learning something, such as say calculus or chemistry. Sometimes we need to learn on-the-fly, meaning that there is a time crunch involved.

The learning can be unsupervised or it can be supervised. Inside the escape room, suppose the other person was so intent on finding clues that they did not explain to you what they were doing. All you had to go on was the aspect that the person was fervently looking around the room. In that sense, you learned they were looking for clues and did so in an unsupervised manner, namely the person did not guide you or explain what to learn. If the other person had told you that you needed to start looking for clues, and then perhaps told you to look behind the painting hanging on the wall and look under the desk, this would be more of a supervised kind of learning.

Back to the Machine Learning aspects, there is a trade-off of having to do supervised versus unsupervised learning. It could be that if the ML is supervised and given direction and pointers, it will have a better learning outcome, but this also requires usually added effort and cost versus the unsupervised approach. In the escape room, for every moment that the other person tries to tell you what to do, it perhaps is depriving them of seeking to find clues and aid the escape, therefore there is a "cost" involved in their supervising you versus if they had not done so.

Another factor involves what you already know and how your prior knowledge plays into what you are trying to learn anew.

Suppose my children had already known something about wolves. Perhaps they had seen cartoons on the Saturday morning TV shows that depicted wolves. These might have been simply cartoon-like wolves. Upon seeing the picture of an actual wolf, which I showed them along with the picture of the coyote, they now could connect together the actual wolf picture with the cartoon images of wolves they had already seen. In that case, they were leveraged in the learning because they already had prior background that was useful to the item they were newly learning.

175

Once you've done an escape room challenge, the odds are that the next time you do one, you'll be more proficient. Furthermore, it might also mean that when you do the second one, you'll be able to learn new tricks about how to escape a room, which layers onto the tricks you learned from the first time you did an escape room. Our prior foundation of what we know can be a significant factor in how well and how fast we can learn something new.

There are numerous attempts underway of trying to find ways to improve Machine Learning and Deep Learning to be able to do one-shot or few-shots kind of learning.

For example, the Siamese neural network is a variant on the use of neural networks that tries to deal with the one-shot goal. Taking its name from the concept of Siamese twins, you have two (or more) neural networks that you setup and train in the same manner. They are twins. You then have a conjoining element which is going to measure the "distance" of their outputs in terms of whether their outputs are considered quite similar versus being quite dissimilar.

Using a pair-wise comparison technique, you can use the Siamese neural network to compare two (or more) inputs and try to determine if they are likely the same or different. Let's say I provide a picture of a dog and a cat. Based on a numeric vector that is output from each of the two neural networks, one receiving the dog picture and the other receiving the cat picture, the conjoining distance estimator would hopefully indicate that there is a large numeric difference between the outputs, which suggests the cat is not the same as the dog.

Another promising approach involves augmenting a Deep Neural Network with external memory. These Memory Augmented Neural Networks (MANN) leverage the connected external memory as a means to avoid various kinds of difficulties associated with neural networks that are being retrained. There is a chance during retraining of inadvertently "forgetting" prior aspects, of which, the external memory can potentially make-up for that deficiency.

There are other approaches such as the Hierarchical Bayesian Program Learning (HBPL) and other kinds of Bayesian one-shot algorithms that are being explored. One of the most popular datasets used in examining one-shot learning consists of using the famous Omniglot dataset, which consists of various handwritten characters and involves trying to do handwriting recognition from a sparse set of exemplars.

Efforts to seek one-shot learning are ongoing and eagerly are sought so as to reduce the burden involved in having to gather lots of exemplars, plus, it is hoped or assumed that the lesser number of exemplars needed will also reduce the amount of learning time needed.

Humans seem to have a capacity to do one-shot learning. It is not always perfect and people can readily learn "the wrong thing" based on a one-shot approach. Nonetheless, it seems to be a crucial cognitive capability and one that we humans depend upon greatly.

What does this have to do with AI self-driving cars?

At the Cybernetic AI Self-Driving Car Institute, we are developing AI software for self-driving cars. One aspect that we are exploring involves the use of one-shot learning for AI self-driving cars.

Allow me to elaborate.

I'd like to first clarify and introduce the notion that there are varying levels of AI self-driving cars. The topmost level is considered Level 5. A Level 5 self-driving car is one that is being driven by the AI and there is no human driver involved. For the design of Level 5 self-driving cars, the auto makers are even removing the gas pedal, brake pedal, and steering wheel, since those are contraptions used by human drivers. The Level 5 self-driving car is not being driven by a human and nor is there an expectation that a human driver will be present in the self-driving car. It's all on the shoulders of the AI to drive the car.

For self-driving cars less than a Level 5, there must be a human driver present in the car. The human driver is currently considered the responsible party for the acts of the car. The AI and the human driver are co-sharing the driving task. In spite of this co-sharing, the human is supposed to remain fully immersed into the driving task and be ready at all times to perform the driving task. I've repeatedly warned about the dangers of this co-sharing arrangement and predicted it will produce many untoward results.

Let's focus herein on the true Level 5 self-driving car. Much of the comments apply to the less than Level 5 self-driving cars too, but the fully autonomous AI self-driving car will receive the most attention in this discussion.

Here's the usual steps involved in the AI driving task:

- Sensor data collection and interpretation
- Sensor fusion
- Virtual world model updating
- AI action planning
- Car controls command issuance

Another key aspect of AI self-driving cars is that they will be driving on our roadways in the midst of human driven cars too. There are some pundits of AI self-driving cars that continually refer to a utopian world in which there are only AI self-driving cars on the public roads. Currently there are about 250+ million conventional cars in the United States alone, and those cars are not going to magically disappear or become true Level 5 AI self-driving cars overnight.

Indeed, the use of human driven cars will last for many years, likely many decades, and the advent of AI self-driving cars will occur while there are still human driven cars on the roads. This is a crucial point since this means that the AI of self-driving cars needs to be able to contend with not just other AI self-driving cars, but also contend with human driven cars. It is easy to envision a simplistic and rather unrealistic world in which all AI self-driving cars are politely interacting with each other and being civil about roadway interactions. That's not what is going to be happening for the foreseeable future. AI self-driving cars and human driven cars will need to be able to cope with each other.

Returning to the topic of one-shot learning, let's consider how this kind of learning comes to play with AI self-driving cars.

When you first learned to drive a car, the odds are that much of what you learned was new to you, though it occurred within the context of a lot of other things that you already knew. You did not wake-up one morning with an empty noggin and suddenly find yourself sitting in the driver's seat of a car. Instead, you brought to your learning about how to drive a car the various prior experiences of life and dealing with all kinds of aspects of being in this world.

For example, no one needed to likely explain to you that there are these things called streets and that cars can drive on them. I'd bet that you already knew this before you opted to turn the key and start the engine. You knew that there are other cars on the roadways. You knew that cars can go fast and they can go slow. You knew that there are turns to be made and various rules-of-the-road are to be observed and abided by. You likely had been a passenger in a car, many times before, and knew somewhat the nature of the act of driving. And so on.

Imagine if we found one of those hidden-in-the-jungle humans that has never had contact with the outside world, and we opted to put them behind the wheel of a car. They'd have no particular knowledge about streets, cars, and all of the rest of those aspects. It would be a steep learning curve for them to cope with how to drive a car. I don't know of any such situations wherein someone from the hidden jungles has suddenly been asked to drive a car, and so for now let's assume that by-and-large most people learned to drive a car when they already had a lot of prior knowledge generally about cars and what happens when you drive a car.

You typically learn to drive a car over an extended period of time, perhaps weeks or months in duration. With my children, I would take them to an empty parking lot at a mall, and they'd drive round and round for an hour or so. We'd do this repeatedly, a few days a week. Gradually, we'd build up towards trying to drive in the local neighborhood, doing so when the streets were relatively empty. After a while, I'd have them drive into community traffic situations and get used to that kind of driving. Eventually, we worked-up the nerve to go onto the crazed freeways at high speeds.

In terms of AI for self-driving cars, one of the key problems is that unlike humans, the AI we're starting with has no semblance of what a teenager has about the nature of the world around them. The AI is like the hidden-in-the-jungle human, since it has essentially no background or prior knowledge per se about cars, streets, and all the rest. I would assert that the AI is even worse off than the human from the jungle, since the human from the jungle presumably has cognitive capabilities and we could likely readily teach the person about the nature of streets, cars, etc.

For Machine Learning aspects, the primary focus to-date in AI for self-driving cars has been the processing of sensory data. When the AI receives sensory data, the data needs to be analyzed to ascertain what it has to indicate about the world surrounding the self-driving car. There are visual images coming from the cameras and image processing needs to occur in an effort to ferret out whether there is a car ahead and whether there are pedestrians in the roadway. The same kind of sensory processing needs to be done for the radar, the LIDAR, the ultrasonic sensors, and any other kind of sensory devices on the self-driving car.

Somehow, we need to have the AI system "learn" to find in that sensory data the aspects needed to then be able to properly and safely drive the car. This involves being able to extract from the massive amounts of sensory data the elements that are important to be considered.

Where is the street ahead?

Where are other cars?

Are those cars coming toward the self-driving car or away from it? Are there any potential collisions that might happen? Etc.

Let's use the aspect of road signs to consider the kind of learning involved. We might setup a Deep Neural Network that we feed with thousands upon thousands of pictures of road signs for training purposes. This includes stop signs, caution signs, deer crossing signs, and so on. We are seeking to have the Machine Learning be able to find the patterns associated with each of these signs and therefore be able to spot it when we capture images from the cameras on the AI self-driving car.

Assuming we've done a good job of training the neural network, we'll go ahead and include it into the on-board system of the AI self-driving car. Sure enough, when images are being fed from the cameras, the on-board neural network is crunching the image data and able to ascertain that it found say a stop sign. The sensory analysis portion of the AI system doesn't especially act on the fact that it found a stop sign and merely passes this detection onward to the other processes of the AI system (it is up to the AI Action Planning portion to ascertain what to do about the detected stop sign, such as issuing car commands to bring the car to a stop).

Once we've loaded-up the neural network into the on-board system, we're going to freeze it from learning anything new, which we might do because we're concerned that if it was allowed to continue to "learn" while in-the-wild that it might learn the wrong things. We are worried that it could somehow change from considering stop signs of being stop signs to instead interpreting stop signs to be merely caution signs (in which case, this would be passed along to the AI Action Planner, which would not likely bring the car to a stop since it has been misinformed about the nature of the posted sign).

One of the problems with not allowing the Deep Neural Network to learn "on the fly" is that it might encounter posted signs it has not yet seen and thus not try to figure out what the sign signifies. It might simply report that there is an unknown sign up ahead and let the AI Action Planner figure out what to do about it.

I remember one time while my children were still novice drivers that we came up to a quite unusual road sign (one that I had not seen before either). The road sign said, "Turn Right to Go Left." What's that? Seemingly an oxymoron. But, it actually did make sense due to the aspect that there was a kind of dog leg to the right that curved back and around a partial roundabout, allowing you to ultimately go to the left, which otherwise you could not directly make a left turn legally.

It was the kind of roadway sign that you figure won't make-or-break you, meaning that it wasn't a life or death kind of matter. If you didn't notice the sign, it meant that you would not be able to make a rather immediate left and would need to go down another block to make a left turn. When I first spotted the sign, I looked and could see that some drivers either did not see the sign or ignored it, and they proceeded up a block to make a desired left turn.

With further pride in my heart, I watched as my novice driver detected the road sign, offering a bit of a startled look about it, carefully judged what it meant, and opted to make the right in order to make the left. This was done smoothly and without any apparent confusion. I would also bet that in the future, if such a sign was ever detected again, it would be a natural now for my child to know what it intended.

I'd say it was a one-shot learning instance. The roadway sign was detected, interpreted, utilized, and now has become part of the repertoire of road signs known by my offspring.

What would an AI self-driving car do?

Assuming it had not already been trained on such a road sign, which I'd wager was unlikely to be in a normal training dataset, the Deep Neural Network would have likely detected that the sign existed, and would have identified where it was positioned, but otherwise would not have been able to categorize what the sign was. It would certainly indicate that it was probably not a stop sign, and not a caution sign, and not a deer crossing sign, and so on. It would be considered unlike those signs and instead be a sign that was unknown as to what was intended by the sign.

The AI Action Planner could take a chance and assume that the sign had no significance to the driving task at-hand. Suppose the AI Action Planner was hoping to turn left. It might opt to do what I had seen some other humans do, namely just proceed up a block and then make a normal left turn. In that manner, the AI got kind of lucky that the sign wasn't something more onerous like "Abyss in 5 Feet" or something like that.

If possible, it would be handy if the AI system could learn on-the-fly and have figured out the meaning of the road sign. My novice teenage drivers were able to do so.

Essentially, we need to have one-shot learning for AI self-driving cars. I'd also go with the possibility of zero-shot learning and the few-shots learning. Any of those would be quite handy.

In this case, it was not a life or death kind of situation, but there might be such circumstances that the AI could encounter, and for which the lack of a one-shot learning mechanism might lead to complications or even injuries or deaths. I realize that some AI developers balk at my example and say that if the data from the self-driving car is being fed to the cloud of the auto maker or tech firm, using OTA (Over The Air) electronic communications, the cloud-based system might have been able to better interpret the newly encountered road sign and then push back into the AI self-driving car the aspects of what to do.

Realistically, it is not likely that the OTA would have had sufficient time to transmit the data, have the data crunched someplace in the cloud, devise an indication of what the sign meant, and then push down a patch into the AI self-driving car. That's some kind of magic we don't yet have.

Sure, ultimately, the hope is that the cloud-based systems will be collecting tons of data from fleets of AI self-driving cars, and that the cloud collected data will be analyzed and then "learnings" about the driving task will be shared among the fleet of cars. This though is something that will take days or maybe weeks of the system analyzing these large volumes of data. Plus, the odds are that the AI developers will need to be in-the-loop as part of the analysis and ascertaining what makes sense to add as "new learnings" into the on-board AI of the self-driving cars in their fleet.

Here's then where we are at on this topic. The bulk of the core "learning" for driving a self-driving car is most likely going to take place before the self-driving car gets onto the roadway. It will have the core essentials of the driving task.

Once it is on the roadway, we want the AI to have the capability to do one-shot learning so that it can hopefully better cope with the driving task.

The one-shot learning is likely to occur in real-time. Therefore, there is a severe time constraint involved.

We are only likely to get one exemplar and not have the luxury of somehow having dozens or hundreds of them in-hand (there weren't any other "Turn Right to Go Left" signs anywhere nearby and none that I had ever seen before in my many miles of driving).

The AI is going to need to "learn" in a likely unsupervised setting. There is nothing or no one around that can guide or explain to the AI what the one-shot signifies.

You might suggest that the AI could ask the passenger in the self-driving car and find out if the passenger knows what the sign means. Yes, this might be possible via the use of a Natural Language Processing (NLP) interface with the occupants of the self-driving car. But, suppose there are only small children that are occupants and they don't have any clue about driving or road signs.

Or, maybe the occupants misinterpret the road sign and tell the AI that it needs to make a radical right turn immediately. Should the AI obey such a suggestion? Also, you need to consider that it might be somewhat disconcerting to the occupants that the AI has no clue what the sign says. I suppose you would weigh this reveal against the chances that the road sign is important and might lead to harming or killing the occupants, and thus revealing that the AI doesn't know what the sign means might be a last-gasp attempt to avoid calamity.

Much of the one-shot learning being researched by AI developers focuses on image recognition.

This makes sense as image processing is a usage that we can all readily agree has potential value. If you are doing facial recognition, it would be better to do a one-shot learning over having to get a multitude of pictures of someone's face. Humans seen to be able to see a person's face one time, and then have a remarkable ability to pick that face out of a crowd, even though they may only have seen the face that one time and perhaps even a long time ago.

For an AI self-driving car, having one-shot learning for the sign recognition as an image processing only solution is not quite sufficient. The rest of the AI driving tasks need to also become "learned" about what the sign means. The AI Action Planner won't have any set of driving aspects that apply to the newly detected sign and yet it is the part of the AI processing that must decide what driving tasks to next take, due to detecting the sign.

Thus, the one-shot learning has to permeate across the entire set of AI tasks being undertaken while driving the self-driving car. This is a much harder problem to deal with. If you only were dealing with being able to "recognize" the sign and categorize it, the question becomes what category to apply it to, and does the AI Action Planner have anything ready to do when encountering this potential new category.

A rather significant downside of any one-shot learning will be whether what has been learned in "correct" or not. I mentioned earlier that we might have a Machine Learning that pattern matches that any four-legged animal is a dog, and therefore classify cats as dogs. Suppose the AI on-board the self-driving car is able to do one-shot learning and in the case of this turn right to turn left sign, the AI "learns" that it should come to a stop and then try to make a left.

You might be shaking your head and asking why in the world would the AI "learn" that based on the sign it should come to a stop and try to make a left turn?

Suppose that the AI self-driving car witnesses a human driven car up ahead that does just that, and the AI then falsely assumes that the posted sign and the action of that other car were correlated to each other.

It might then henceforth assign the action of making a stop and an immediate left as the appropriate action when encountering the turn right to turn left sign.

This is the kind of difficulty associated with doing one-shot learning and doing so on-the-fly.

It has rather obvious and potentially adverse consequences on the safety of the AI self-driving car and what it might do.

Conclusion

One-shot Machine Learning and its close cousins are a vaunted goal of AI.

There is still plenty of exploration and research to be done on this topic.

It is handy to pursue because it will not only hopefully improve the capabilities of Machine Learning, it would seem likely that it will force us to further figure out how humans do one-shot learning. The more we can crack the egg of how humans think, it is a good bet that the more we have a chance of getting AI to be imbued with human-like intelligence.

Next time that you are trying to learn something, consider how many exemplars you need to figure out the matter.

Our approach today of needing thousands upon thousands of exemplars for ML and DL does not seem like a viable way to always approach learning.

Depending upon the foundation you are starting with, it should potentially allow you to leverage that basis and possibly do sensible and on-target one-shot learning. I think about this all the time and especially when I see a platypus.

.

APPENDIX

APPENDIX A

TEACHING WITH THIS MATERIAL

The material in this book can be readily used either as a supplemental to other content for a class, or it can also be used as a core set of textbook material for a specialized class. Classes where this material is most likely used include any classes at the college or university level that want to augment the class by offering thought provoking and educational essays about AI and self-driving cars.

In particular, here are some aspects for class use:

o   Computer Science. Studying AI, autonomous vehicles, etc.

o   Business. Exploring technology and it adoption for business.

o   Sociology. Sociological views on the adoption and advancement of technology.

Specialized classes at the undergraduate and graduate level can also make use of this material.

For each chapter, consider whether you think the chapter provides material relevant to your course topic. There is plenty of opportunity to get the students thinking about the topic and force them to decide whether they agree or disagree with the points offered and positions taken. I would also encourage you to have the students do additional research beyond the chapter material presented (I provide next some suggested assignments they can do).

RESEARCH ASSIGNMENTS ON THESE TOPICS

Your students can find background material on these topics, doing so in various business and technical publications. I list below the top ranked AI related journals. For business publications, I would suggest the usual culprits such as the Harvard Business Review, Forbes, Fortune, WSJ, and the like.

Here are some suggestions of homework or projects that you could assign to students:

a) <u>Assignment for foundational AI research topic</u>: Research and prepare a paper and a presentation on a specific aspect of Deep AI, Machine Learning, ANN, etc. The paper should cite at least 3 reputable sources. Compare and contrast to what has been stated in this book.

b) <u>Assignment for the Self-Driving Car topic</u>: Research and prepare a paper and Self-Driving Cars. Cite at least 3 reputable sources and analyze the characterizations. Compare and contrast to what has been stated in this book.

c) <u>Assignment for a Business topic</u>: Research and prepare a paper and a presentation on businesses and advanced technology. What is hot, and what is not? Cite at least 3 reputable sources. Compare and contrast to the depictions in this book.

d) <u>Assignment to do a Startup</u>: Have the students prepare a paper about how they might startup a business in this realm. They must submit a sound Business Plan for the startup. They could also be asked to present their Business Plan and so should also have a presentation deck to coincide with it.

You can certainly adjust the aforementioned assignments to fit to your particular needs and the class structure. You'll notice that I ask for 3 reputable cited sources for the paper writing based assignments. I usually steer students toward "reputable" publications, since otherwise they will cite some oddball source that has no credentials other than that they happened to write something and post it onto the Internet. You can define "reputable" in whatever way you prefer, for example some faculty think Wikipedia is not reputable while others believe it is reputable and allow students to cite it.

The reason that I usually ask for at least 3 citations is that if the student only does one or two citations they usually settle on whatever they happened to find the fastest. By requiring three citations, it usually seems to force them to look around, explore, and end-up probably finding five or more, and then whittling it down to 3 that they will actually use.

I have not specified the length of their papers, and leave that to you to tell the students what you prefer. For each of those assignments, you could end-up with a short one to two pager, or you could do a dissertation length paper. Base the length on whatever best fits for your class, and the credit amount of the assignment within the context of the other grading metrics you'll be using for the class.

I mention in the assignments that they are to do a paper and prepare a presentation. I usually try to get students to present their work. This is a good practice for what they will do in the business world. Most of the time, they will be required to prepare an analysis and present it. If you don't have the class time or inclination to have the students present, then you can of course cut out the aspect of them putting together a presentation.

If you want to point students toward highly ranked journals in AI, here's a list of the top journals as reported by *various citation counts sources* (this list changes year to year):

o   Communications of the ACM

o   Artificial Intelligence

o   Cognitive Science

o   IEEE Transactions on Pattern Analysis and Machine Intelligence

o   Foundations and Trends in Machine Learning

o   Journal of Memory and Language

o   Cognitive Psychology

o   Neural Networks

o   IEEE Transactions on Neural Networks and Learning Systems

o   IEEE Intelligent Systems

o   Knowledge-based Systems

GUIDE TO USING THE CHAPTERS

For each of the chapters, I provide next some various ways to use the chapter material. You can assign the tasks as individual homework assignments, or the tasks can be used with team projects for the class. You can easily layout a series of assignments, such as indicating that the students are to do item "a" below for say Chapter 1, then "b" for the next chapter of the book, and so on.

a) What is the main point of the chapter and describe in your own words the significance of the topic,

b) Identify at least two aspects in the chapter that you agree with, and support your concurrence by providing at least one other outside researched item as support; make sure to explain your basis for disagreeing with the aspects,

c) Identify at least two aspects in the chapter that you disagree with, and support your disagreement by providing at least one other outside researched item as support; make sure to explain your basis for disagreeing with the aspects,

d) Find an aspect that was not covered in the chapter, doing so by conducting outside research, and then explain how that aspect ties into the chapter and what significance it brings to the topic,

e) Interview a specialist in industry about the topic of the chapter, collect from them their thoughts and opinions, and readdress the chapter by citing your source and how they compared and contrasted to the material,

f) Interview a relevant academic professor or researcher in a college or university about the topic of the chapter, collect from them their thoughts and opinions, and readdress the chapter by citing your source and how they compared and contrasted to the material,

g) Try to update a chapter by finding out the latest on the topic, and ascertain whether the issue or topic has now been solved or whether it is still being addressed, explain what you come up with.

The above are all ways in which you can get the students of your class involved in considering the material of a given chapter. You could mix things up by having one of those above assignments per each week, covering the chapters over the course of the semester or quarter.

As a reminder, here are the chapters of the book and you can select whichever chapters you find most valued for your particular class:

<u>Companion Book By This Author</u>

Advances in AI and Autonomous Vehicles:
Cybernetic Self-Driving Cars

Practical Advances in Artificial Intelligence (AI)
and Machine Learning
by
Dr. Lance B. Eliot, MBA, PhD

<u>Chapter Title</u>

This title is available via Amazon and other book sellers

Companion Book By This Author

Self-Driving Cars:
"The Mother of All AI Projects"

by Dr. Lance B. Eliot, MBA, PhD

This title is available via Amazon and other book sellers

Companion Book By This Author
Innovation and Thought Leadership
on Self-Driving Driverless Cars
by Dr. Lance B. Eliot, MBA, PhD

This title is available via Amazon and other book sellers

Companion Book By This Author

New Advances in AI Autonomous Driverless Cars Self-Driving Cars

by Dr. Lance B. Eliot, MBA, PhD

This title is available via Amazon and other book sellers

Companion Book By This Author

Introduction to
Driverless Self-Driving Cars

by Dr. Lance B. Eliot, MBA, PhD

Chapter Title

This title is available via Amazon and other book sellers

Companion Book By This Author
Autonomous Vehicle Driverless
Self-Driving Cars and Artificial Intelligence
by Dr. Lance B. Eliot, MBA, PhD

Chapter Title

This title is available via Amazon and other book sellers

Companion Book By This Author

Transformative Artificial Intelligence Driverless Self-Driving Cars

by Dr. Lance B. Eliot, MBA, PhD

This title is available via Amazon and other book sellers

Companion Book By This Author

Disruptive Artificial Intelligence
and Driverless Self-Driving Cars

by Dr. Lance B. Eliot, MBA, PhD

Chapter Title

This title is available via Amazon and other book sellers

Companion Book By This Author

State-of-the-Art
AI Driverless Self-Driving Cars

by Dr. Lance B. Eliot, MBA, PhD

This title is available via Amazon and other book sellers

Companion Book By This Author

Top Trends in
AI Self-Driving Cars
by Dr. Lance B. Eliot, MBA, PhD

This title is available via Amazon and other book sellers

Companion Book By This Author

AI Innovations and Self-Driving Cars

by Dr. Lance B. Eliot, MBA, PhD

Chapter Title

1 Eliot Framework for AI Self-Driving Cars

2 API's and Self-Driving Cars

3 Egocentric Designs and Self-Driving Cars

4 Family Road Trip and Self-Driving Cars

5 AI Developer Burnout and Tesla Car Crash

6 Stealing Secrets About Self-Driving Cars

7 Affordability and Self-Driving Cars

8 Crossing the Rubicon and Self-Driving Cars

9 Addicted to Self-Driving Cars

10 Ultrasonic Harm and Self-Driving Cars

11 Accidents Contagion and Self-Driving Cars

12 Non-Stop 24x7 and Self-Driving Cars

13 Human Life Spans and Self-Driving Cars

This title is available via Amazon and other book sellers

<u>Companion Book By This Author</u>

Crucial Advances for
AI Self-Driving Cars

by Dr. Lance B. Eliot, MBA, PhD

<u>Chapter Title</u>

This title is available via Amazon and other book sellers

Companion Book By This Author

Sociotechnical Insights and AI Driverless Cars

by Dr. Lance B. Eliot, MBA, PhD

This title is available via Amazon and other book sellers

Companion Book By This Author

Pioneering Advances for AI Driverless Cars

by Dr. Lance B. Eliot, MBA, PhD

This title is available via Amazon and other book sellers

Companion Book By This Author

Leading Edge Trends for
AI Driverless Cars

by Dr. Lance B. Eliot, MBA, PhD

This title is available via Amazon and other book sellers

Companion Book By This Author

The Cutting Edge of
AI Autonomous Cars

by Dr. Lance B. Eliot, MBA, PhD

<u>Chapter Title</u>

This title is available via Amazon and other book sellers

Companion Book By This Author

The Next Wave of AI Self-Driving Cars

by Dr. Lance B. Eliot, MBA, PhD

Chapter Title

This title is available via Amazon and other book sellers

Companion Book By This Author

Revolutionary Innovations of AI Self-Driving Cars

by Dr. Lance B. Eliot, MBA, PhD

Chapter Title

This title is available via Amazon and other book sellers

AI Self-Driving Cars
Breakthroughs

by Dr. Lance B. Eliot, MBA, PhD

Companion Book By This Author

Trailblazing Trends for **AI Self-Driving Cars**

by Dr. Lance B. Eliot, MBA, PhD

Chapter Title

This title is available via Amazon and other book sellers

<u>Companion Book By This Author</u>

Ingenious Strides for
AI Driverless Cars

by Dr. Lance B. Eliot, MBA, PhD

<u>Chapter Title</u>

This title is available via Amazon and other book sellers

Companion Book By This Author

AI Self-Driving Cars Inventiveness

by Dr. Lance B. Eliot, MBA, PhD

This title is available via Amazon and other book sellers

ABOUT THE AUTHOR

Dr. Lance B. Eliot, MBA, PhD is the CEO of Techbruim, Inc. and Executive Director of the Cybernetic AI Self-Driving Car Institute, and has over twenty years of industry experience including serving as a corporate officer in a billion dollar firm and was a partner in a major executive services firm. He is also a serial entrepreneur having founded, ran, and sold several high-tech related businesses. He previously hosted the popular radio show *Technotrends* that was also available on American Airlines flights via their in-flight audio program. Author or co-author of a dozen books and over 400 articles, he has made appearances on CNN, and has been a frequent speaker at industry conferences.

A former professor at the University of Southern California (USC), he founded and led an innovative research lab on Artificial Intelligence in Business. Known as the "AI Insider" his writings on AI advances and trends has been widely read and cited. He also previously served on the faculty of the University of California Los Angeles (UCLA), and was a visiting professor at other major universities. He was elected to the International Board of the Society for Information Management (SIM), a prestigious association of over 3,000 high-tech executives worldwide.

He has performed extensive community service, including serving as Senior Science Adviser to the Vice Chair of the Congressional Committee on Science & Technology. He has served on the Board of the OC Science & Engineering Fair (OCSEF), where he is also has been a Grand Sweepstakes judge, and likewise served as a judge for the Intel International SEF (ISEF). He served as the Vice Chair of the Association for Computing Machinery (ACM) Chapter, a prestigious association of computer scientists. Dr. Eliot has been a shark tank judge for the USC Mark Stevens Center for Innovation on start-up pitch competitions, and served as a mentor for several incubators and accelerators in Silicon Valley and Silicon Beach. He served on several Boards and Committees at USC, including having served on the Marshall Alumni Association (MAA) Board in Southern California.

Dr. Eliot holds a PhD from USC, MBA, and Bachelor's in Computer Science, and earned the CDP, CCP, CSP, CDE, and CISA certifications. Born and raised in Southern California, and having traveled and lived internationally, he enjoys scuba diving, surfing, and sailing.

ADDENDUM

AI Self-Driving Cars Inventiveness

Practical Advances in Artificial Intelligence (AI) and Machine Learning

By
Dr. Lance B. Eliot, MBA, PhD

———

For supplemental materials of this book, visit:
www.ai-selfdriving-cars.guru

For special orders of this book, contact:
LBE Press Publishing
Email: LBE.Press.Publishing@gmail.com